INNOVATION
TOURNAMENTS

INNOVATION
TOURNAMENTS

CREATING AND SELECTING
EXCEPTIONAL OPPORTUNITIES

CHRISTIAN TERWIESCH
KARL T. ULRICH

HARVARD BUSINESS PRESS

Boston, Massachusetts

Library of Congress Cataloging-in-Publication Data

Terwiesch, C. (Christian)
     Innovation tournaments : creating and selecting exceptional opportunities /
  Christian Terwiesch, Karl Ulrich.
        p.   cm.
     Includes bibliographical references and index.
     ISBN 978-1-4221-5222-5 (hardcover : alk. paper)
     1. Technological innovations—Management. 2. Creative ability in business.
  I. Ulrich, Karl. II. Title.
  HD45.T3984 2009
  658.4'063—dc22

                                                                2008043325

CONTENTS

Innovation is often compared to lightning or flying sparks—spontaneous and uncontrollable. Although randomness and serendipity clearly play a role in innovation, and no single analytical tool can innovate for you, we believe that the innovation process can be managed effectively by using a set of scientific principles and analytical tools. This book is a guide to the key scientific principles that underlie successful innovation. We aspire to provide solid frameworks and methods for mastering innovation, supported by logic and empirical evidence.

Our motivation for this approach to innovation arises from our professional backgrounds. We have invented products, started companies, and helped hundreds of companies innovate more effectively. But in what sometimes feels like a double life, we have also taught ten thousand MBA students about process flows, bottlenecks, and quality improvement processes. In a sense, we have been innovators trapped in the bodies of operations management professors. This book harmonizes our two passions—innovation and process management. Our goal is to push readers to apply the rigorous approaches they bring to operations, marketing, and finance to the management of innovation.

Our interest in developing a rigorous approach to innovation goes back to our research in the pharmaceutical industry. Several years ago we began collaborating with Merck & Co. and were struck by the high degree of structure in the drug discovery process. We had little understanding of the underlying medicine, chemistry, and biology, but that turned out to be a blessing. Our ignorance forced us to view Merck's innovation activities abstractly, as a process, with molecular compounds characterized only as "opportunities" flowing through a sequence of innovation phases. As we worked with Merck to improve its process, we became convinced that innovation in many sectors, even intrinsically creative ones like movies and music, could be approached using the process view.

The notion of an *innovation process* presents an apparent contradiction: innovation is fundamentally concerned with creating new things, but a process does the same things repeatedly. This contradiction is resolved by viewing the process at the right level of abstraction. For most of this book, we will focus on the concept of an *opportunity*. In pharmaceuticals, the opportunity is a newly discovered chemical compound. In Hollywood, it's the story line for a movie. For a consumer-products company, it might be a newly expressed customer need, perhaps in response to new information about health. For a venture capital firm, it's a business plan submitted by a start-up. Within an organization, each opportunity differs in terms of the specific need addressed or solution deployed, but a set of standard actions can apply to managing these opportunities within the innovation process. Movie scripts may differ in their characters and plots, but the process of creating a movie can be broken down into a standardized sequence of innovation phases—script development, preproduction, production, and so forth. Indeed, when viewed as a process for managing a collection of opportunities, innovation looks very similar across sectors, whether those sectors are movies, pharmaceuticals, consumer goods, or venture capital.

Don't misread us. We are not arguing for a standardization of the fine structure of innovation tasks. Passion, creativity, art, and serendipity will continue to play critical roles in the creation of value. Our argument is that when abstracted sufficiently, the management of opportunities on which innovation tasks are focused can be some-what standardized and systematized. A key challenge is to derive the benefits of this standardization without limiting the potential for creative magic at the level of the individual innovation project.

The major benefit of taking the process view of innovation is that it supports performance measurement, analysis, and process improvement. Rigor transformed the management of production in the twentieth century. We believe a similar rigor can transform the management of innovation in the twenty-first century.

This book is aimed at managers who are responsible for profit growth through innovation. This is the audience we have been working with for many years in our innovation management executive programs at the Wharton School. We find that no single job title fits this group but that its members face common challenges. These managers may work in several different places in organizations. Some are general managers of business units and chief executives. Some work in staff business development roles. Others work in product development or R&D organizations. Still others have line management roles in marketing or operations. In addition, we have used much of the material in the book successfully in our project-based MBA and executive education courses on innovation management.

Some of the material in this book is challenging analytically. We debated whether to include this material, given that some of our target readers will not find it accessible. We took the approach of including any material we believe is really important and that we feel has not been adequately covered in existing books. To draw on an analogy, the best financial managers do not shy away from analytically sophisticated approaches when maximizing value. The management of innovation is no less important and warrants the understanding and application of tools and frameworks that make a difference, whether or not those tools and frameworks require intellectual effort.

We expect to improve these materials over time, so we very much welcome your feedback and suggestions. The Web site that accompanies this book, www.InnovationTournaments.com, will reflect your input, containing updates and supplemental materials as they become available.

To us, innovation is the most interesting and fun organizational pursuit. We hope this book will help you achieve exceptional results as you seek to improve the innovation process in your organization.

—Christian Terwiesch
Karl T. Ulrich
Philadelphia, November 2008

INTRODUCTION

Innovation can make fortunes. A robust return on equity for a large firm is 20 percent per year. Contrast this with the returns for these innovations:

⟹ Zocor, Merck's cholesterol drug, has contributed gross profits of well over $10 billion on an investment of about $500 million.[1]

⟹ Apple sold more than 100 million iPod portable music players in just the first six years after the portable music player's 2001 introduction. The iPod and the online iTunes store have generated over $30 billion in revenue for Apple. Remarkably, Apple spends a *lower* percentage of revenue on research and development than most of its competitors.[2]

⟹ The movie *Harry Potter and the Sorcerer's Stone* had a budget of about $125 million. Five years after launch, it had created over $1 billion in revenues for Warner Brothers

Studios. The creator of the Harry Potter saga, author J. K. Rowling, has seen an even greater payoff. She has become a billionaire thanks to books, movies, and merchandise based on Harry's adventures.

Harry Potter and the Sorcerer's Stone brought Warner Brothers Studios in excess of $1 billion. How did other Warner Brothers movies launched during the same period fare? Remember *Chasing Liberty* or *The Big Bounce*? Or how about *Exorcist: The Beginning*? If not, don't worry—you aren't alone. Few people saw them, and the studio made little if any money on those projects. Moreover, when Warner Brothers was making *Harry Potter*, it also analyzed thousands of other pitches for movies, developed hundreds of scripts, and seriously considered launching another dozen or so movies. Few of them made it to the box office, much less made money.

For Warner Brothers, or any studio, phenomenal successes such as *Harry Potter* are the exception. But for a successful innovator, *exceptions* are the goal. In this book, we aim to guide you through the intelligent management of the creation, selection, and development of exceptional opportunities for innovation.

In the game of innovation, no bet comes with a guarantee. But that doesn't mean you can't become a better player. Recently two Serbians and a Hungarian won $2 million from the Ritz Casino in London.[3] Luck? Robbery? Or simply smart betting? Perhaps all three. They allegedly used a laser embedded in a mobile phone to scan the velocity of the ball when the croupier released it and sent this data to a remote location. Based on historical data on a given croupier and a simulation model of the physics of the ball, a computer recommended bets. Could this approach perfectly forecast the outcome? No, but it could improve the odds from the traditional 37:1 to 6:1. In other words, by making use of historical data, professional methods, and a clever process, a fool's game became a profitable business. Minus the chicanery, this is the logic underlying this book. Innovation will always remain risky. Many projects will fail,

and most opportunities won't warrant substantial investment. However, by following the tools, principles, and methods in this book, you
can shift the odds in your favor.

WHAT WE MEAN BY INNOVATION

We define *innovation* broadly as a *new match between a need and a
solution*. The novelty can be in the solution or the need—or in a new
marriage of an existing need and an existing solution. Zocor was a
new solution coming out of Merck's research labs that addressed the
existing need to protect against heart disease. The recent introduction of the Smart car in the United States by the German automotive
company Daimler is an example of applying an existing solution (the
vehicle was introduced in Germany in 1997) to the newly emerging
need for fuel-efficient vehicles in a country where gasoline was historically very inexpensive. The iPod was a new match between an existing need and an existing solution. The first iPod used disk drive
technology very similar to what was inside most notebook computers
at the time, and it addressed the existing need for the portable storage
and playback of digital music, a need that was previously addressed
by MP3 players using flash memory.[4]

This definition of innovation encompasses hardware, software, services, and processes as well as needs that are found anywhere, whether
in a factory, a consumer marketplace, or the public arena. A new way
to reduce heat loss in an office building to improve its energy efficiency
could be an innovation, and so could the redesign of a manufacturing process to utilize a new automation technology. Thus, innovation
need not always lead to new products or new lines of business.

In addition to achieving a new match between a need and a solution, *successful* innovation creates value. In most commercial settings, this means that the innovation results in financial profits, but
alternative notions of value such as social welfare or environmental
protection may motivate innovation in other settings.

Opportunities Beget Innovations

We define an *opportunity* as the seed that might later grow into an innovation. An opportunity is an innovation in embryonic form, a newly sensed need, a newly discovered technology, or a rough match between a need and a possible solution. At this early stage of development, uncertainty clouds future value, so an opportunity can be thought of as a *hypothesis* about how value can be created. For a pharmaceutical company such as Merck, an opportunity might be a new chemical compound that appears to control blood sugar. For a consumer-products company such as Procter & Gamble, it might be a new cleaner suggested by a customer. For a materials company such as 3M, it might be a new polymer with unusual properties. Some opportunities ultimately become innovations, whereas others might never warrant substantial development.

Four examples of opportunities appear in figures I-1 through I-4. The first (figure I-1) is the creation of an e-mail or text-messaging

---

FIGURE I-1

An opportunity articulated via the Web-based innovation network Cambrian House.

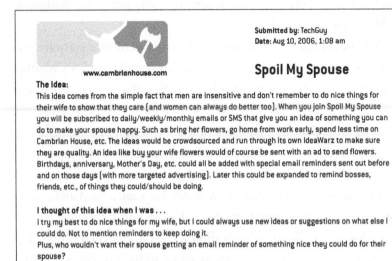

Source: The Cambrian House, http://www.cambrianhouse.com.

FIGURE I-2

An opportunity for a do-it-yourself wireless doorbell. The icons in the lower right refer to the firm's assessment of the opportunity relative to four criteria: its novelty, patentability, development risk, and gross margin potential.

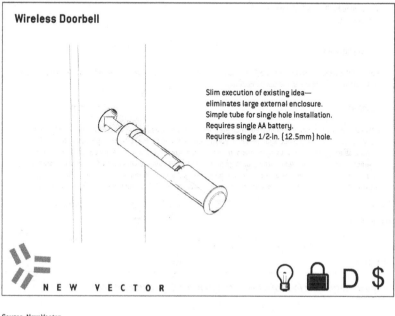

Wireless Doorbell

Slim execution of existing idea—
eliminates large external enclosure.
Simple tube for single hole installation.
Requires single AA battery.
Requires single 1/2-in. (12.5mm) hole.

N E W   V E C T O R

Source: New Vector.

system to remind you to pamper and praise your spouse, while also providing suggestions on how to do this. The second (figure I-2) is a do-it-yourself wireless doorbell. The third (figure I-3) is the script summary for a new movie, and the last one (figure I-4) is an opportunity based on recent nanotechnology research. Note that in all four cases, the creator could describe the opportunity on a single slide, sometimes by combining text and graphics.

SPENDING MORE IS NOT THE KEY TO SUCCESSFUL INNOVATION

Recently the *Financial Times* ranked the fifty most innovative companies, using R&D spending as its measure of innovativeness (figure

FIGURE I-3

An opportunity for a movie, articulated as a script synopsis.

"Deadly Greed"

Screenplay by Robert C. Johnson
October 2006

Screenplay elements:

Movie of the Week (MOW) or Feature Film / Humor / Romance / Environmental Theme / Dog / Suspense / New York / Idaho / Family Movie / Black Screenplays

Synopsis:

A NY tycoon and his wife are murdered. Their son, Jeff, a drunken loser and new CEO, is stressed to the max by corporate murders and betrayal. He and a stray mutt hit the road in a ratty pickup truck and he hides his identity as a logger for a company he owns in a small Idaho town. Jeff discovers the corrupt company's interested only in forest clear-cutting for huge profits and rules over the workers and distrustful community. Corporate NY murders continue, and a hit man takes his best shot at eliminating Jeff. But newfound love, a disabled boy's courage, and a dog's devotion and sacrifice save Jeff from himself and the enemy within.

Source: Robert C. Johnson.

FIGURE I-4

An opportunity in the form of a new result from a U.S. government laboratory.

Carbon nanotubes for eliminating die swell

NIST research in *Nature Materials*, August 2004

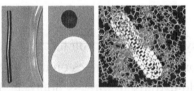

Researchers at the National Institute of Standards and Technology (NIST) have discovered that the addition of carbon nanotubes to a common commercial polymer, polypropylene, leads to dramatic changes in how the molten polymer flows. This process eliminates a widespread manufacturing headache known as "die-swell" in which polymers swell in undesirable directions when passing through the exit port of an extruder.

Researchers have been adding small amounts of nanotubes—tiny tubes of carbon about 1,000 times thinner than a human hair—to polypropylene in hopes of dramatically enhancing the material's strength and other properties. Once realized, this enhanced polymer could be processed at high speed through extruders for use in manufacturing.

NIST materials scientists were concerned that because nanotubes make the polypropylene rubbery, the material would be difficult to process or its enhanced properties would be lost. To their surprise, the opposite proved true. When sheared (forced) between two plates, the polymer normally separates the plates. However, when nanotubes are added, the plates are pulled together. The scientists discovered that this "pulling-together" completely alleviated die-swell. Industry currently uses various time-consuming trial-and-error solutions to deal with the problem. Eliminating die-swell should help manufacturers improve their time-to-market by simplifying their die design processes and enabling the controlled manufacture of smaller components.

Source: National Institute of Standards and Technology. Reprinted from *NIST TechBeat*.

I-5). According to its scorecard, the more a company spent, the more innovative it was. The fact that Ford, General Motors, and Daimler-Chrysler made it into the top four of the ranking must have left the editors puzzled.

You most likely will agree that one should not measure the innovativeness of a company by only looking at how much it spends on R&D. How about looking at the financial returns that are generated by the R&D investment? Do companies that spend more on innovation in the form of R&D outlays perform better financially? Consider the data in figure I-6, based on an analysis of R&D spending in the computer industry.[5] The horizontal axis of the graph shows

FIGURE I-5

The Financial Times *R&D scorecard was derived from data from the U.K. Department of Business, Enterprise, and Regulatory Reform (DBERR).*

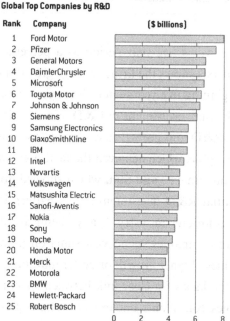

Global Top Companies by R&D

Rank	Company	($ billions)
1	Ford Motor	
2	Pfizer	
3	General Motors	
4	DaimlerChrysler	
5	Microsoft	
6	Toyota Motor	
7	Johnson & Johnson	
8	Siemens	
9	Samsung Electronics	
10	GlaxoSmithKline	
11	IBM	
12	Intel	
13	Novartis	
14	Volkswagen	
15	Matsushita Electric	
16	Sanofi-Aventis	
17	Nokia	
18	Sony	
19	Roche	
20	Honda Motor	
21	Merck	
22	Motorola	
23	BMW	
24	Hewlett-Packard	
25	Robert Bosch	

The initial study was done by the U.K. Department of Trade and Industry. The exhibit shows just the top twenty-five of the fifty firms.

Source: Department for Business, Enterprise, and Regulatory Reform, "The Top Global Companies by R&D, Growth and R&D Intensity," DBERR Web site, http://www.innovation.gov.uk/rd_scoreboard/world_global.asp.

FIGURE I-6

The relationship between R&D spending as a percentage of revenues and revenue growth five years later.

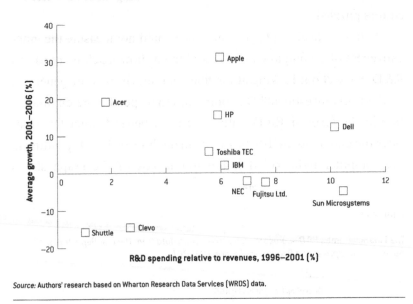

Source: Authors' research based on Wharton Research Data Services (WRDS) data.

R&D spending over a five-year period as a percentage of revenue, and the vertical axis shows the firms' average growth rate for the five-year period beginning five years later. Some companies achieved little growth with scant investment in R&D. No surprise there. Others spent more on R&D and grew faster. No surprise there, either. The riddles include Apple, which achieved the fastest growth with below-average R&D investment, and Sun, which showed no growth at all, despite substantial R&D investments. This pattern is by no means unique to the computer industry. Many chemical, pharmaceutical, and automotive companies spend vast sums on innovation, yet do not seem to achieve higher growth or better margins.[6]

Based on the lack of a clear link between spending and performance, academics, consultants, and executives have questioned whether investments in innovation create value.[7] The absence of an obvious connection between spending and financial returns suggests that you cannot improve your financial performance by blindly increasing your investment in innovation. But it does not imply that investments in innovation cannot be profitable. As we mentioned previously, the iPod has generated over \$30 billion in revenue for Apple, and substantial profits. Unlike many innovations introduced by Apple's competitors, the iPod was created with relatively little investment. The iPod neither required a lot of R&D spending (it used an existing technology) nor a lot of spending to educate consumers (it served an existing need). A key to Apple's success was that it focused its investment on an opportunity with exceptional profit potential. In the balance of this chapter, we relate exceptional opportunities to financial performance using a tool we call the return curve, and then we show how innovation tournaments, the central framework for this book, are used to find such opportunities.

THE INNOVATION RETURN CURVE

Underlying the analysis in figure I-6 is a simplistic view of innovation that treats innovation like a black box. You pour money in at one end and hope that more of it gushes out the other end. This approach assumes that increased innovation spending benefits all organizations, without accounting for the specific opportunities that would benefit from additional investment. The fallacy in this assumption is revealed by looking at the reality of the investment decisions faced by most organizations.

Most opportunities exhibit a similar financial profile—you invest money now with the hope that you will receive more money later. Consider the seven opportunities which could receive investment listed in table I-1. For each opportunity listed, values are estimated for the required investment (A) and expected profit contribution (B). A profitability index (C) is calculated simply as the ratio of profit contribution to required investment (B/A). The net profit contribution (D) is simply the expected profit contribution less the required investment (B – A). The cumulative profit contribution (E) is the sum

TABLE I-1

Seven hypothetical opportunities for investment.

	A	B	C	D	E
	Required investment	Expected profit contribution	Profitability index	Net profit contribution	Cumulative profit contribution
Opportunity	($ millions)	($ millions)	(B/A)	(B − A)	(sum of D's)
1 Redhook	5	53	10.6	48	48
2 Chocorua	3	22	7.3	19	67
3 South Street	22	90	4.1	68	135
4 Myth Buster	11	22	2.0	11	146
5 Carlos	5	7	1.4	2	148
6 Muriel	14	14	1.0	0	148
7 Idaho	9	8	0.9	−1	147

of the net profits contributed by the opportunities, assuming they are pursued in the order listed.

We find it useful to represent this same information in a graphical form we call a *return curve* (figure I-7). Each opportunity is shown as a rectangle whose width represents the required investment and whose height represents the expected profitability index. These rectangles are placed from left to right in order of profitability. The area under the curve and above a profitability index of 1.0 represents the profits (above and beyond the cost of capital) that the firm expects to earn from these projects.[8]

Executives face tough choices regarding how much to invest in innovation and which opportunities to pursue. We suspect that executives studying these opportunities would devote the bulk of their time to Carlos, Muriel, and Idaho—that is, the marginal opportunities at the bottom of table I-1. Redhook, Chocorua, South Street, and Myth Buster promise such high payoffs that they are no-brainers and can be moved forward with little discussion. Carlos, Muriel, and Idaho, in contrast, are the ones that require long meetings in which proponents make the weak case for funding. They eat up management attention during development, because they're always teetering on the edge of termination.

FIGURE I-7

The return curve graphically represents the expected profits from a set of investments. Each opportunity for investment is shown as a rectangle whose width is the size of the required investment and whose height is its profitability.

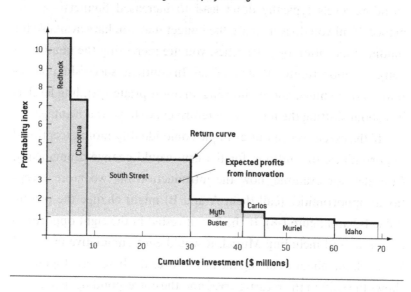

The unfortunate reality is that managers focus too much of their attention on marginal opportunities and aim most of their sophisticated analytical tools at discerning subtleties in these opportunities. Exceptional opportunities—those that will account for the majority of profits—are not marginal; they are clearly superior. We believe that instead of obsessing over marginal opportunities, you're better off considering how you can increase the supply of exceptional opportunities.

Exceptional Opportunities Drive Exceptional Value

Although some individual innovations can have fantastic returns, simply spending more on innovation overall does not necessarily lead to increased profits. Consider the Time Warner example again. In any given year, the studio faces a certain number of movie projects. Some of them, like *Harry Potter*, are exceptional and offer amazing financial returns. However, such projects are rare, and a simple increase in investment is more likely to fund another *Chasing Liberty* or *The Big Bounce* than to deliver another *Harry Potter*.

The return curve provides an explanation for why increased spending levels typically don't lead to increased financial performance. If all you do is increase the budget that you have available for funding innovation opportunities, you are increasing the number of marginal opportunities that you fund. In contrast, successful innovation is not so much about choosing an appropriate spending level as it is about shifting the innovation return curve to your advantage.

If the executives in our example could identify more exceptional opportunities, the outlook for the firm would change dramatically. Consider, for example, how the introduction of two more exceptional opportunities (call them A and B) might change the picture (table I-2 and figure I-8). If the firm invested in the eight opportunities up to and including Muriel, it would earn cumulative profits of $280 million, about doubling the profits over the base case. Figure I-9 shows the shift in the return curves and the corresponding increase in profits.

TABLE I-2

The original seven opportunities plus two exceptional opportunities.

	A	B	C	D	E
Opportunity	Required investment contribution ($ millions)	Expected profit ($ millions)	Profitability index (B/A)	Net profit contribution contribution (B − A)	Cumulative profit (sum of D's)
A Exceptional Opp A	8	104	13.0	96	96
1 Redhook	5	53	10.6	48	144
B Exceptional Opp B	4	40	10.0	36	180
2 Chocorua	3	22	7.3	19	199
3 South Street	22	90	4.1	68	267
4 Myth Buster	11	22	2.0	11	278
5 Carlos	5	7	1.4	2	280
6 Muriel	14	14	1.0	0	280
7 Idaho	9	8	0.9	−1	279

FIGURE I-8

The return curve shifts dramatically with the creation of two new exceptional opportunities.

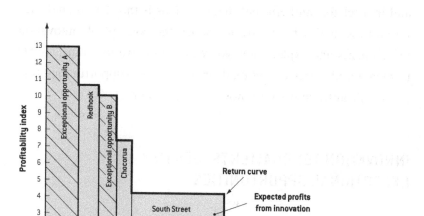

FIGURE I-9

Comparing the original and new return curves illustrates the potential increase in profit expected as a result of the two new exceptional opportunities available to the firm.

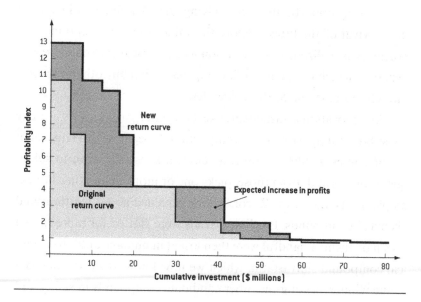

Of course, adding hypothetical opportunities to the spreadsheet is easy. How can such exceptional opportunities be identified in practice and in a reliable and efficient manner? This is the central challenge we address in this book. We introduce the concept of innovation tournaments and explain how you can use innovation tournaments to create and select exceptional opportunities—opportunities that can significantly shift your innovation return curve.

INNOVATION TOURNAMENTS IDENTIFY EXCEPTIONAL OPPORTUNITIES

Creating opportunities is sometimes compared with lightning or flying sparks—spontaneous and uncontrollable.[9] Although randomness and serendipity clearly underlie the fate of any particular opportunity, we believe that deliberate management of a system we call an *innovation tournament* can introduce professional rigor to the innovation process, the same rigor you likely apply in other parts of your business, whether financial budgeting or supply chain management.

At the most basic level, an innovation tournament is a competition among opportunities, embodying the Darwinian principle of the survival of the fittest. Before the value from an exceptional opportunity is realized, at its inception as a chemical cocktail in a petri dish or a sketch on a napkin, it competes with many other opportunities to become one of the chosen few.

An innovation tournament, like its counterpart in sports, usually consists of multiple rounds of competition. It begins with a large set of opportunities. A filtering process selects a subset to move to subsequent rounds and, from those, picks one or more champions. For example, in its search for Zocor, Merck screened about ten thousand chemical compounds. Preclinical trials were started for more than a dozen of them; a handful were then tested in humans until the chemical compound simvastatin, which we now know as Zocor, emerged as the winner, beating the other candidate compounds in safety and efficacy.

Innovation tournaments characterize consumer product innovation as well. Figure I-10 reflects the process used to find the handle for the Oral-B cross-action toothbrush. The exhibit shows the dozens of foam models that Oral-B's designers built and the five molded prototypes that it tested with consumers. Consumers liked the design shown in the middle of the photo best, and the innovation enabled Oral-B to redefine the premium segment of the manual-toothbrush market.

Whether organizing opportunities for pharmaceuticals or toothbrushes, all innovation tournaments have a similar structure, summarized in figure I-11. A large number of opportunities enter the tournament as contestants. A sequence of filtering steps (three in the case of figure I-11) eliminates most opportunities, leaving only the ones with the promise of exceptional value as survivors.

FIGURE I-10

The development of the Oral-B cross-action toothbrush involved the structured exploration of dozens of forms. Lunar Design's designers prototyped and tested five concepts (shown in the center of image) before selecting the final design.

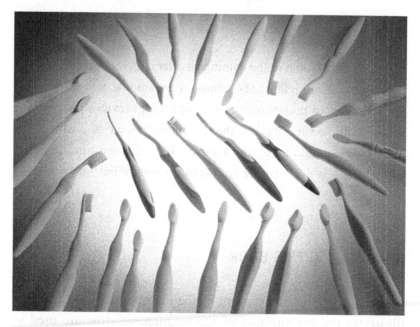

Source: Lunar Design.

FIGURE I-11

Tournaments begin with a relatively large number of "contestants" and apply filters in a series of rounds in order to identify "winners." Effective innovation tournaments result in exceptional opportunities.

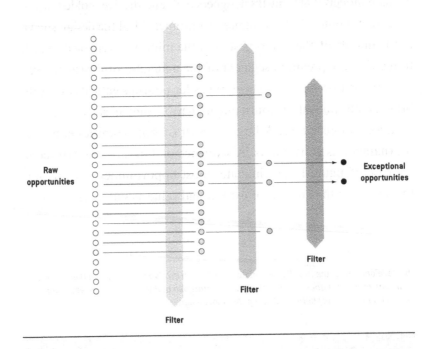

As you will learn in the coming chapters, several versions of this basic tournament design are common. For example, you might allow opportunities to mutate, to bounce back to a previous phase, or to spawn multiple variants. Yet, the fundamental logic of creation and filtering is common to all tournaments. Indeed, the central question of this book is not whether to use tournaments but rather how to manage them.

ROAD MAP TO THIS BOOK

Chapter 1 develops the concept of the innovation tournament and illustrates the key variants of the tournament structure used in practice. It also identifies the key levers on performance within the tournament structure.

Chapter 2 discusses tools and techniques that help you generate many more opportunities. It discusses ways to harness the power of individuals and groups in that quest. Chapter 3 shows how to sense opportunities that arise outside of your organization, thus increasing the number of opportunities competing in your innovation tournaments.

Chapter 4 discusses the first elimination round in a tournament. At this stage, the challenge is primarily one of handling a large number of opportunities. You'll screen for those with the highest potential, and only the most promising opportunities will pass into the later rounds.

Chapter 5 explains how to align an organization's innovation tournaments with its business strategy so that the opportunities you identify are more likely to address gaps in your innovation portfolio.

Innovation opportunities are worthless without intelligent filtering. In the second half of the book, we provide ways to improve your bets in each round of your tournaments. Chapter 6 explains how to analyze each opportunity in detail, using financial models of uncertain payoffs. Chapter 7 broadens the focus from individual opportunities to entire innovation portfolios and discusses how to deal with company growth expectations, resource constraints, interdependencies among opportunities, and diversification of risk. Chapter 8 offers strategies for managing the cultivation and development of the most risky, but also potentially the most profitable, opportunities.

Once you have decided to implement an innovation tournament, you face a host of questions. How many filters should you impose? How quickly should you reduce the number of opportunities? How many raw opportunities should you consider in the first round? Chapter 9 guides you in designing the shape and size of a tournament to suit your business needs. Chapter 10 then discusses the organization of tournaments, suggesting different approaches for governance and administration. It also addresses when and how you should take advantage of ideas from outside the organization.

We conclude with a chapter on getting started, which helps you obtain some quick wins from applying innovation tournaments in your organization. We explain how to analyze your existing innovation process and help you set up your first innovation tournament.

TOURNAMENTS 101

A Primer for Innovators

To illustrate the nuts and bolts of a tournament, consider the reality television show *American Idol.* One of the most popular shows on TV, it has attracted an audience of over 30 million people and has been replicated around the globe. Every season, it starts with a tour of a handful of American cities, where tens of thousands of wannabe stars audition in front of juries. Only about a hundred from each city get a second audition, this time in front of a larger jury. That group is then winnowed down to forty, who head to Hollywood. There, each performs a song from a given list and another of his or her choice and participates in various group performances. Finally, the best twenty-four contestants strut and sing weekly in the television series, where the audience votes for the best one. A principal goal of the show is to entertain viewers, in part through the public humiliation that is typical in the early rounds. Nevertheless, the process is astounding in its ability to start with hordes of apparently undistinguished people and identify artists who go on to win Grammys and even an Academy Award.[1]

American Idol resembles an innovation tournament: many contestants compete, but only the fittest survive. In this chapter, we explain innovation tournaments and show you how companies use them. We lay out the management levers available to improve your innovation tournaments and position tournaments within the larger context of innovation management and product development.

FOUR EXAMPLES OF INNOVATION TOURNAMENTS

The professional services organization Deloitte conducts an annual innovation tournament. The objective of this tournament is to identify the innovative ideas occurring every day at client sites or field operations, to bring them to the core of the organization for incubation and development, and then to deliver them back to the edge so that more clients or personnel benefit from them. The tournament, which Deloitte refers to as Innovation Quest, also fosters an ongoing culture of innovation.

Deloitte's innovation tournament includes three phases: ideation, collaboration, and evaluation. In the ideation phase, all 43,000 employees of Deloitte are invited to submit ideas electronically. Innovation leaders and subject-matter experts from relevant disciplines within the organization review and select ideas to move to the next phase. In the collaboration phase, idea owners build a team and solicit feedback on their ideas. Feedback is obtained from a diverse set of backgrounds available in the organization, leading to a significant enhancement of the initial proposals. During the final phase, evaluation, all Deloitte personnel are encouraged to provide their views on the most promising concepts—they vote for the best ideas—which is a significant factor in determining the winners.

To date, more than one thousand ideas have been submitted to Deloitte's Innovation Quest, and more than ninety individual winners have been named. Winners received monetary rewards and gained exposure to senior leadership. Among the winning ideas were a new enterprise sustainability service, which allows clients to measure, improve, and sustain their social and environmental performance, and a new talent management suite, consisting of solutions designed to enhance an organization's ability to attract, develop, engage, and retain talent.

Just as Deloitte looks for innovations in professional services, so Dow Chemical seeks them in its factories. For more than a decade, Dow has held an annual innovation tournament on how to save energy and reduce waste. Factory staff, never going higher than the supervisor level, are encouraged to submit project ideas that pay for themselves within one year and cost less than $200,000 to implement. Submissions are peer reviewed, and the most promising projects are implemented. Employees receive substantial cash prizes, and Dow reports triple-digit returns from these improvement projects.[2] In fact, an audit of 575 projects that resulted from this tournament revealed average returns of 204 percent and an annual savings of $110 million.

As a third example, consider Innocentive, a company that organizes innovation tournaments so that its customers, typically large technology-based companies, can overcome specific technical challenges. Innocentive publicizes a problem to a broad audience, including academics like us, experts like you, and anyone else who's interested. These people then submit their proposed solutions to Innocentive (typically along with some supporting scientific evidence), and Innocentive and its customer pick one or more winners. Winners get cash, and the customer surmounts its challenge.

Innovation tournaments also underlie the creative works of architects and designers, as our fourth example illustrates. Figure 1-1 shows the logo designs considered for TerraPass, a service that allows consumers to offset the carbon dioxide emissions from their autos, air travel, and homes. The logo chosen by the company—at the far right in the figure—has worked brilliantly. Yet it did not come about

FIGURE 1-1

The innovation tournament leading to the TerraPass logo started with hundreds of concepts, of which twenty-three were tested. Additional concepts were developed around the circulating-arrow theme in the first round of the tournament. Ultimately the design at the far right prevailed.

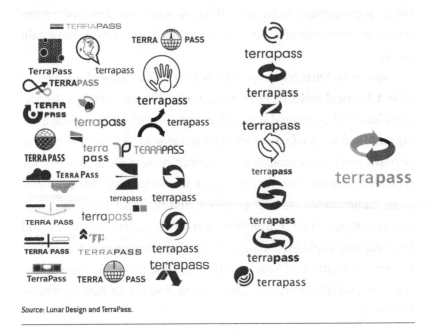

Source: Lunar Design and TerraPass.

in a single creative flash. It beat out dozens of competing concepts, which company managers had created with the help of professional designers. The final logo was picked in an innovation tournament.

DISTINGUISHING ATTRIBUTES OF INNOVATION TOURNAMENTS

New services for Deloitte, manufacturing improvements at Dow, solutions to scientific puzzles, or a new logo for a startup—regardless of the goal, the basic structure of an innovation tournament is always the same. All tournaments start with a set of contestants, which correspond to opportunities for innovation. Opportunities are then filtered to find the one (or the few) that is most likely to result in substantial value.

Beyond this common structure, however, innovation tournaments can exhibit significant differences. This section outlines key attributes that characterize different types of tournaments.

Is the Tournament Open or Closed?

Open tournaments are run in public, and anyone may enter. Open tournaments have driven innovation throughout history. In the 1700s, the British government offered awards for discoveries in navigation and the measurement of time. In the 1800s, the French Academy offered 100,000 francs to the person who could produce soda from seawater. In the early 1900s, the Orteig Prize offered a $25,000 purse for completing the first nonstop flight from New York to Paris. Nine teams competed, and Charles Lindbergh won by crossing the Atlantic in 1927 in his *Spirit of St. Louis* airplane. In the early twenty-first century, Mojave Aerospace Ventures received a $10 million award from the X-Prize Foundation for flying its *SpaceShipOne* into orbit with a budget that was a fraction of prior government-sponsored efforts. And, most recently, U.S. presidential candidate John McCain outlined plans to award $300 million to the organization that can leapfrog current battery performance while simultaneously reducing production cost.

The organizer of an open tournament is often a public body such as a government or nonprofit group, but, as Innocentive demonstrates, profit-seeking companies can serve that role, too.[3] The strength of open tournaments is that they attract a broad range of participants, leading to a large, diverse set of opportunities. Witness Lindbergh. Before his famed flight, the press of the day had characterized him as a daredevil and an amateur—a "flying fool" who was sure to die in his attempt. His single-engine/single-pilot strategy departed radically from the conventional thinking of the time; thus, a more orthodox aviator, sponsored by a government or a large company, probably would not have tried it.[4]

Most innovation tournaments operated by companies, however, are *closed*. Employees identify the opportunities, and the firm keeps the proceedings proprietary. Deloitte's Innovation Quest and Dow's tournament both operate this way.

Is the Tournament a Pure Cascade or Does It Allow Renewal and Iteration?

Most athletic tournaments are *pure cascades* in which contestants are evaluated and either advance or are eliminated. Pharmaceutical companies usually conduct their tournaments as pure cascades. Each opportunity—in their case, newly discovered chemical compounds— either advances or is eliminated. Once eliminated, a compound does not get a second chance.

A tournament can also be *iterative,* however, allowing the initial opportunities to spawn others or letting eliminated ones be improved and then reentered in the competition. Notice how Deloitte uses the collaboration phase in its tournament not just to filter opportunities but also to enhance them. Similarly, the final version of the Terra-Pass logo was not a contestant in the first round of that tournament. It evolved from one of the initial ideas, which also used the theme of the two intertwined arrows. Figure 1-2 illustrates the concept of iteration in the form of additional arrows (going from right to left) and additional opportunities that appear only after the first filter has been applied.

Does the Tournament Play Out in One or Multiple Rounds?

The simplest tournament consists of one round, resembling a running race like the New York Marathon. Thousands of opportunities compete in the single round of evaluation, and the best prevail. Often, however, innovation tournaments consist of multiple rounds, resembling the playoff structure of sporting events such as Wimbledon in tennis or the World Cup in soccer. Multiround tournaments

FIGURE 1-2

A tournament with renewal and iteration. A new opportunity is identified after the first filter, an opportunity is refined and reemerges as a first-round candidate, and an opportunity spawns two variants.

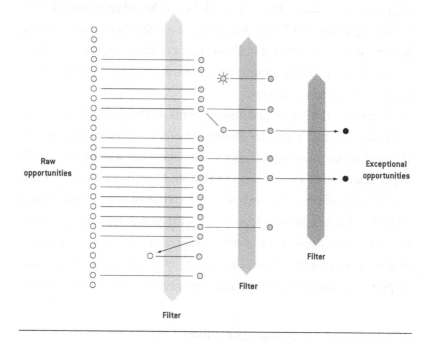

quickly weed out the mediocre opportunities, making it possible to devote more time and resources to evaluating the most promising ones.

Remember the search by Oral-B's designers for a better toothbrush, which we described in the introduction to this book? The designers created about a hundred sketches in round 1 and dozens of foam models in round 2, and then tested just five plastic prototypes with consumers in round 3. Similarly, Deloitte uses two phases of evaluation and voting in its Innovation Quest.

Does the Tournament Employ Absolute or Relative Filters?

A tournament can employ absolute or relative standards to judge opportunities. With an absolute standard, opportunities are evaluated against a fixed benchmark or threshold of quality. If an innovation clears the threshold, it advances. In contrast, a relative standard operates like a beauty contest: the best opportunity wins, not because of its absolute worth, but because it beats the other entries. To win the Orteig Prize, Lindbergh had to meet an absolute standard. Had he landed in Brest, on France's western coast, he would have flown further than any prior contestant but would not have met the criterion and received the money.

Similarly, the innovation tournaments at Deloitte and Dow seek opportunities that meet the absolute standard of promising profits. If, in any given tournament, one of the companies identified multiple opportunities that seemed to meet that standard, it would most likely not restrict itself by funding just one. In contrast, a tournament that seeks a novel design for a logo or a toothbrush is typically based on relative comparison. Even if the organizer finds several promising designs, it will only use one. Conversely, even if none of the designs inspires awe, the best of them may advance for further development.

Which Innovation Tournament Is Right for Me?

Open or closed, cascading or iterative, one round or multiple rounds, absolute or relative comparisons. Which is right for you? And how do you run *your* tournament, ensuring that *your* opportunities are exceptional and create economic value? These questions are at the heart of this book. In answering them and related questions, we'll articulate a principle-based approach to the efficient creation, selection, and development of opportunities—the science of innovation tournaments.

THE POWER OF TOURNAMENTS

At first glance, tournaments appear to be a wasteful way of innovating. They require you to invest time and money in generating many opportunities only to abandon most of them. If innovation were a manufacturing process, it would have horrible levels of defects. Indeed, tournaments are the *second-best* way to innovate. A better approach is innovation based on rigorously tested scientific theories. If, for example, you had a scientific model that would let you create the perfect song for a particular market segment, including its rhythm, melody, and harmonies, your job as a music producer would be easier. You'd just crank up the computer and let it sing. In some fields, innovators have such models. Aircraft engineers at Boeing or Airbus don't need a tournament to find the size of the fuel tanks required to supply an airplane intended to cross the Atlantic.

In practice, most innovation problems don't allow that sort of approach. Instead, aspiring innovators have to rely on a certain amount of trial-and-error exploration to find exceptional opportunities.[5] The lack of science is especially vexing for areas in which consumer tastes alone determine the fate of an innovation, as in the world of entertainment. Think about movie production. Studios such as Pixar do not find blockbusters like *Cars* based on scientific theories. Several years before making the animated feature, the company considered about five hundred pitches, each describing a potential movie (figure 1-3). The story line for *Cars* sprang from neither a random flash of inspiration nor an analytical process based on published theories of movie making and consumer preferences. Instead, it was the outcome of an innovation tournament.

For every individual opportunity you consider, whether molecule, movie pitch, or mousetrap, you face a range of possible outcomes and thus uncertainty regarding the payoffs of the opportunity. When you create opportunities, you essentially print lottery tickets. To use terminology from statistics, you create *draws from a payoff distribution*. There is little harm associated with a ticket that does not win; the *winning* tickets in your pocket are the only ones you care about. In innovation tournaments, these winning tickets are the exceptional opportunities that create the bulk of the financial value from innovation.

FIGURE 1-3

The feature film Cars *arose from a tournament that began with about five hundred candidate pitches.*

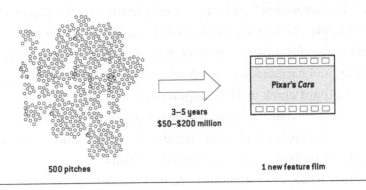

3–5 years
$50–$200 million

Pixar's *Cars*

500 pitches   **1 new feature film**

Figure 1-4 illustrates the opportunity creation process and the logic of seeking exceptional opportunities.[6] The process creates a stream of raw opportunities, which you filter for quality. Imagine the filter as a hurdle over which only the best opportunities must pass. The process will probably produce many middling opportunities for every exceptional one. We illustrate this variance in the quality of the created opportunities with a bell-shaped curve. Great ideas are scarce and lie out on the upper tail of the payoff distribution.

Given that the best opportunities are rare, how can you increase the supply of ones that clear your quality hurdle? How can you print more winning lottery tickets? There are three basic ways.

1. Increase the *average quality* of your opportunities. If you create better ones on average, more will clear the hurdle.

2. Increase the *quantity* of your opportunities. If you produce more opportunities, you'll see more exceptional ones. The logic here is simple: on average, if you find one seven-foot-tall person per hundred thousand people, you'll find two among two hundred thousand. Creating more opportunities (without sacrificing their average quality) is thus a key lever in finding the exceptional few.

FIGURE 1-4

The opportunity creation process. The objective of the process is to find a few exceptional opportunities, not to produce consistently middling ones.

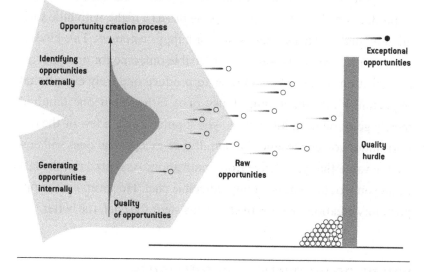

3. Increase the *variance in the quality* of your opportunities. This is a direct, though not immediately obvious, implication of statistics. Holding the average quality and number of opportunities constant, you'll generate more exceptional ones if your process exhibits *greater variability*—that is, if it's *less consistent* in the quality of its output. Variability contradicts normal approaches to process improvement, but it's exactly what you want in opportunity creation. Generating wacky ideas and wild notions increases the chance that at least one of your opportunities will be exceptional.

Not a Six Sigma Process

Many business people have been trained to try to eliminate variability, driving toward highly consistent, repeatable outputs. This is the logic of modern quality management, including the concepts of *process capability* and *Six Sigma*. It also happens to be exactly the wrong way to think about innovation.

If you managed a chain of pizzerias, you'd want each restaurant to produce one hundred tasty, tempting pizzas a night, with little variation in quality. That's what makes for happy customers. This kind of performance would, however, be a terrible outcome for an opportunity creation process. You'd prefer to produce one truly exceptional opportunity and ninety-nine lousy ones rather than one hundred merely good ones. In innovation, you'll pursue only a few of the opportunities you create, and that handful of exceptional ones will create the value that you derive from innovation. As a pizzeria, the last thing you would want is an unpredictable chef. However, for the opportunity creation process, the less consistent the chef, the better.

WHERE DO INNOVATION TOURNAMENTS FIT IN YOUR BUSINESS?

In the past two decades, most firms have structured the *product development* portion of their innovation efforts, often with a *phase-gate* process. These processes have clearly defined phases, usually four or five, with intermediate gates, essentially go/no-go reviews. With most phase-gate processes, the presumption is that the target opportunity, if addressed effectively, will result in a successful product or service. Most of the projects that go into a phase-gate process do eventually come out, and the fraction of projects killed during the process is typically at most half.

The strength of the phase-gate process is that it applies the structure and managerial rigor you are used to from production or sales to the development of new products and services. This activity upstream of the product development process, often labeled "the fuzzy front end," historically has been managed loosely (if at all) and often has been perceived as the work of creative geniuses.

A phase-gate process is not an innovation tournament. Phase gates work well at developing and advancing an opportunity after it is somewhat validated. Once you have identified a great business opportunity such as the iPod, the phase-gate process will help you to develop it. But the phase-gate process does not help you to identify the opportunity of a disk drive–based portable music collection in the first place.

The focus of this book is the sensing, screening, and evaluation that happens before development even begins. Just as the perfect production of a poorly designed product will lead to commercial failure, so will the perfect development of a bad innovation opportunity. The phase-gate process revolutionized product development in many companies by introducing structure and analysis. Now is the time to revolutionize the way you create and select opportunities (figure 1-5).

Other Tournaments in Business

Tournaments are a broad tool. You almost certainly run them in other areas of your business when, for example, searching for a new

FIGURE 1-5

One way to think about the innovation process is as an opportunity tournament that precedes a phase-gate new-product development process.

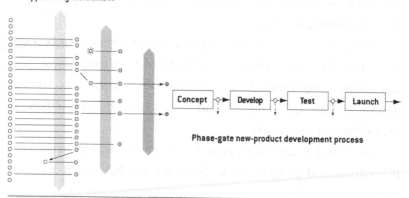

Opportunity tournament

Concept → Develop → Test → Launch →

Phase-gate new-product development process

executive, a new product name, or a new enterprise software system. If you're like us, you might even use tournaments to determine what car to buy or where to spend your next vacation. A lot of the lessons in this book will translate to other tournaments you run. We also readily acknowledge important aspects of innovation that go beyond the management of tournaments. For this reason, not everything in this book is restricted to tournaments.

Thus, this book is about innovation and it's about tournaments. Most of the book is about the use of tournaments in innovation, but some of the ideas about innovation are not unique to tournaments and some of the ideas about tournaments are not unique to innovation. We hope you can accommodate this looseness in these conceptual boundaries.

SUMMARY

Tournaments propel innovation, whether the goal is Lindbergh's advance in aviation or Deloitte's refinement of its professional services. All tournaments start with many opportunities and filter them to identify the exceptional ones.

When running an innovation tournament, you must make a number of organizational decisions. Will your tournament be open or closed? Will it be a pure cascade or allow iteration? Will you have one round of elimination or multiple rounds? Will your quality standard be absolute or relative?

Three levers enable you to improve the quality of your best opportunity, that is, the winner (or winners) of your tournament. You can feed the tournament with a greater number of contestants. You can improve the average quality of your contestants. Or you can increase the variance in their quality.

Innovation tournaments provide a structured way to manage the fuzzy front end of innovation. Not even the best product development process can create exceptional value if you feed it with a mediocre opportunity.

Diagnostics

Each of the ten main chapters in this book concludes with a number of questions that help you to apply the lessons of the chapters to the innovation challenges you face. Because this chapter provided an overview of the idea of innovation tournaments, we begin with broad questions, many of which will be the subjects of future chapters. Please pick an innovation challenge you recently faced and reflect on it.

- How many opportunities did you consider at the outset? Did you consider enough? What would have happened if you'd considered more?

- How did you identify your opportunities? In what way did they reflect your current business strategy? Did you identify them largely by looking inside your company or outside?

- How did you evaluate the opportunities financially? When in the tournament did you start using financial metrics? How did you incorporate risk into your assessments of value?

- How did you determine the stringency of your filters and the ratio of winners to losers at each phase of the tournament?

- How did you compare radical innovations with uncertain prospects to incremental innovations with relatively certain payoffs?

2

IN-HOUSE SOURCES
Generating Opportunities Internally

Most organizations generate about half of the opportunities in their innovation tournaments *internally* through the creative efforts of individuals and teams.[1] This chapter focuses on generating more and better raw opportunities through the efforts of your people. As with many pursuits, you mostly improve at this by working hard. Although we don't know of easy ways to skirt the diligent application of effort, a handful of techniques can get you started and prevent you from getting stuck.

In this chapter, you will learn to

➡ Apply a set of techniques to stimulate opportunity generation

➡ Structure the front end of a tournament to capture ideas from members of your organization

➡ Effectively harness the creative abilities of individuals and groups

These techniques can be used by entrepreneurs seeking business ideas, an executive attempting to revitalize a product line, or a task force exploring new business opportunities for an existing firm.

The approach of this chapter is largely to "push"—to feed the innovation tournament with promising raw material and hope that some of the opportunities fit well with the strategic direction of the organization. However, when working within the context of an existing organization, a "pull" can also be exerted on the opportunity generation process. Chapter 5 is focused on pulling opportunities into the process based on your desired strategic direction.

TECHNIQUES FOR STIMULATING OPPORTUNITY GENERATION

For some creative people there is nothing more fun than coming up with new ideas. However, we find that the majority of people have a hard time when asked simply to generate some promising opportunities. For them the problem of coming up with something new is simply too abstract, too unstructured, and has too many degrees of freedom. To stimulate the generation of many ideas from a diverse group of people, you must provide your employees, especially those struggling with the task, guidance in opportunity generation.

In the following pages, we suggest a collection of methods for generating opportunities. We will explain how you can internally create opportunities by looking for alternative approaches to existing innovations, following a personal passion, taking an annoyance-driven innovation approach, de-commoditizing a commodity, driving an innovation "down market," being trend driven, creating new product attributes, and decomposing the functions of a business in a novel way. Several other authors, including Nalebuff and Ayres and

Shane, offer additional methods.[2] The chapter notes and our Web site, www.InnovationTournaments.com, provide references to this stream of work as well as to Web-based resources for facilitating idea generation.

Alternative Approaches to Existing Innovations

When another firm innovates successfully and brings a new product or service to market, it in effect publishes the location of a gold mine. You can exploit this information by either considering alternative solutions that could address the same need or alternative needs that could be addressed with the same solution. Here's how: (1) Scan the media and monitor the marketing activities of other firms by, say, attending trade shows. (2) Articulate the need and solution associated with any innovation that you identify. (3) Generate alternative approaches to meeting the need or alternative needs that can be addressed with the new approach.

For innovations in many domains, you should scan *WIRED*, *Fast Company*, *Inc.*, the *New York Times*, and the *Wall Street Journal*. Almost any issue of these publications will yield a handful of new innovations. Consider the product review shown in figure 2-1. The need is caffeine delivery (or, more fundamentally, increasing alertness). The solution is dissolvable film strips, originally used by Pfizer in Listerine PocketPaks. Other opportunities easily generated from the identified need include caffeine spray, caffeine jelly beans, and caffeine sweetener packs (mixed with Splenda, perhaps). Other substances that dissolvable strips might be used to deliver include ibuprofen, antihistamines, vitamins, guess-the-flavor medicines, and fluoride.

Follow a Personal Passion

Innovators who have the luxury of considering any field can benefit from plumbing their personal passions. It's easy. List your passions—endeavors that keep you awake with excitement—and then consider

FIGURE 2-1

Boots caffeine strips as described in a magazine.

Fresh Perked
Boots Caffeine Strips; $2; www.boots.com

Joe Wilde
Senior Editor
Venture 2.0

I remember how my father, always in a hurry, used to wish for a way to combine mouthwash and caffeine in one timesaving product. After 20 years, my father's dream has come true: Boots, the largest U.K. pharmacy chain, recently began selling these mint flavored caffeine strips. They're a lot like Listerine breath-freshening strips, but the Boots product also delivers a shot of caffeine that's about equal to half a cup of coffee. (28 strips come in a pack, but Boots recommends using no more than 4 a day.) They're useful when you want a java jolt without having to take a bathroom break later. The buzz hits you immediately. Now, whenever I visit the U.K., a growing list of mates want me to bring back Boots strips for them.

TELL US ABOUT YOUR INDISPENSABLE TOOLS AT favorites@venture2.com

Source: Adapted from *Business 2.0.* Photo courtesy of Nucci Studio.

how emerging technologies, trends, and business models might influence them. Or identify unmet needs that you have in connection with the personal interest. An avid bicyclist whom we know has been developing a nutrient delivery system for use with existing hydration backpacks (for example, Camelbak), which has applications for the military and for a wide variety of sports (figure 2-2). He identified the opportunity while reflecting on his desire to adjust the amount of sugar and electrolytes in the beverages in his pack.

Annoyance-Driven Innovation

Successful innovators are often chronically dissatisfied with the world around them. They notice unmet needs of users, including themselves. Consider Tom Stemberg, founder of Staples, the office-supply company, and later Zoots, a dry-cleaning chain. Stemberg started both because of his frustrations with existing firms. When taking this approach, list every annoyance or frustration you en-

FIGURE 2-2

Nutrient delivery system worn during testing by the inventor, Matt Kressy (nutrient pouch, tubing, and valve are on his right side).

counter over a period of days or weeks and then pick the most universal and vexing ones and dream up solutions. Any problem is an opportunity. An annoyance faced as this paragraph is being written, for example, is that the cable television technician can only be scheduled for four-hour windows during the workweek. Who can wait around for half a day on a Wednesday for the cable technician? How about allowing anyone requiring service to accept or decline actual openings as they come available with, say, thirty minutes' notice? The notice of an opening could be sent by text message to a cell phone, and all you would need to do is reply to the message to accept the opening. You may not find this particular solution compelling. Maybe you've already thought of a better one.

An annoyance that gives birth to an opportunity doesn't have to be yours alone. Instead, you might find it through customer complaints or market research. A powerful way to understand others' annoyances is to immerse yourself into the world of people using your products or services. In chapter 5, we introduce user anthropology as a powerful method to find out first hand from your potential customers what they like about your products or services and what they find annoying.

De-commoditize a Commodity

Often, price competition characterizes a product category, and the offerings themselves are little more than commodities. Recall coffee before Starbucks or breath mints before Altoids. A commodity such as this creates an opportunity for innovation. To pursue this kind of innovation, list all of the inexpensive, undifferentiated products or services in a category and then consider the possibility of deluxe versions. Take all-purpose wheat flour. It's often found on the bottom shelf of the supermarket. Most households use little of it except around holidays. The typical packaging, a paper bag, is messy. Why not sell the flour in a resealable plastic container that could be stored in the freezer to preserve freshness? Perhaps other baking supplies could be sold with compatible packaging. Consumers might be willing to pay a premium for a solution attuned to their needs. Thus, when you are de-commoditizing an existing product, you drive it "up the market" with the goal of increasing the market.

Drive an Innovation Down Market

Just as you can drive products up the market, so you can drive products down the market. Consider the example of four entrepreneurs with a history in the toy and candy businesses. They believed that their competitive advantage was in creating small, cheap, battery-powered devices, as they had done with the Spin Pop, a lollipop spun by a little motor. To generate opportunities for a new venture in 1998, they trolled the aisles at Wal-Mart looking for expensive devices that they could make dramatically cheaper. They were struck by the array of electric toothbrushes available, many selling for about $100, yet none having much more complexity than their spinning lollipops. They decided to "create an electric toothbrush that can sell for six dollars." Their Spinbrush became the best-selling toothbrush of any type in 2000, and they eventually sold their business to Procter & Gamble for about $475 million (figure 2-3).[3] To follow their example, list the premium products or services in a category and then imagine much cheaper versions that provide many of the same benefits.

Driving an innovation down market works well if a product or service is only available to industrial or commercial customers. In this case, you can "consumerize" the offering. Often, innovators introduce a product or service to needy, less-price-sensitive segments, typically commercial or industrial customers. The original innovator may lack the resources or interest to pursue a consumer version, giving rise to an opportunity.

FIGURE 2-3

A Braun electric toothbrush and the Crest SpinBrush. In the 1990s, electric toothbrushes like the Braun model sold for $50 to $100. The target price for the SpinBrush was $6.

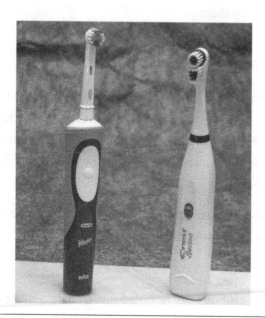

You can explore these sorts of opportunities by pondering a product or service normally provided only to industrial, professional, or commercial markets and then envisioning a consumer version. Energy service consultants, for example, operate in commercial markets. They pay utility bills for clients and work to improve the energy efficiency of clients' operations, sharing the savings with their clients. Given that many homeowners have utility expenses approaching $1,000 per month, why not apply the energy services model to households?

Trend-Driven Innovation

Changes in technology, demography, or social norms often create innovation opportunities. Ubiquitous cellular telephone service, for example, enables a wide variety of information delivery services. An increasing Spanish-speaking population in the United States enables new sorts of Spanish-language media. Growing environmental awareness creates a market for green products and services. Once again, the means of exploration is easy: list social, environmental, technological, or economic trends and then imagine innovation opportunities made possible by them.

Attribute-Based Innovation

Marketers typically think of products and services in terms of their attributes—cars, for example, possess fuel economy, style, speed, and ride quality. You can identify opportunities for differentiated offerings by considering these questions, suggested by Kim and Mauborgne in *Blue Ocean Strategy*:[4]

- Which attributes that are assumed to be required in an industry can be eliminated?

- Which attributes can be reduced substantially?

- Which attributes can be raised substantially above expectations?

⟹ Which attributes can be introduced that are entirely new to the industry?

As an example, consider the attributes of an innovation in the financial services industry. Companies use stock exchanges in their search for additional funding. Often, this means going public. When preparing for an initial public offering, a company might consider using one of several stock exchanges. From the company's perspective, relevant product attributes of stock exchanges include the required minimum capitalization, the exchange services the stock exchange offers, and the prestige of the stock exchange. Figure 2-4 shows how the NASDAQ rates along this set of attributes.[5] This curve is often referred to as a *value curve*.[6]

Figure 2-4 also shows how a recent innovation in the world of financial services stacks up compared with the NASDAQ. The Alternative Investment Market (AIM), created by the London Stock Exchange, is shown relative to the NASDAQ and the OTC Bulletin Board. The AIM does not have the stringent capitalization and revenue requirements of the NASDAQ, yet provides similar exchange services. Because of its location in the United Kingdom, which has fewer securities regulations than the United States, companies pay much less to go public on the AIM. AIM's cheaper stock offerings change the competitive landscape for stock markets.

Functional Decomposition

Innovation opportunities sometimes arise through disturbances to one or a few elements of a business model. You can identify these elements by mapping the functions of the business. Almost any firm can be modeled along the lines of a generic template such as the one depicted in figure 2-5. The firm first acquires customers through sales and marketing and then, through a second process, delivers its product or service to them. These processes can be further broken down into subprocesses.

FIGURE 2-4

An attribute map for stock exchanges. The map compares the relative performance of three stock exchanges across a set of five attributes. The London Stock Exchange Alternative Investment Market innovates by emphasizing the affordability of an initial public offering (IPO), a new attribute for this product category.

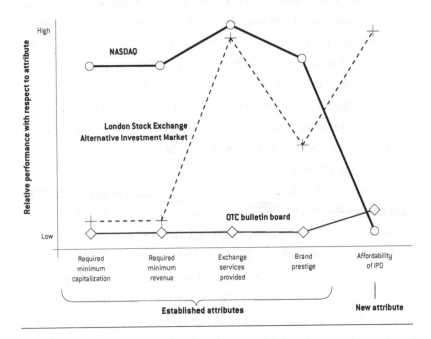

Opportunities for innovation exist at every juncture in the system. An innovator might identify new markets, new sales channels, new ways to locate customers or build relationships with them, or new means of product or service delivery. You zero in on these sorts of opportunities by diagramming the key functions of a business and then considering what would happen if you changed one or more functions. Take the category of fractional jet ownership. NetJets sells shares in an airplane and then operates the aircraft in such a way as to ensure thirty-minute response time to a request by an owner/customer. (This model is shown in the upper part of figure 2-5.) Could NetJets aggregate and coordinate available aircraft across its fleet and resell the capacity as an air-taxi service (see lower part of the figure)?

FIGURE 2-5

An example of a derivative to an existing business. At the top is a high-level decomposition of the business model for the existing NetJets business, consisting of four functions. By changing one or several of the functions underlying the current business model, you create a new business model. At the bottom of the figure is one opportunity generated in this way, an air taxi service.

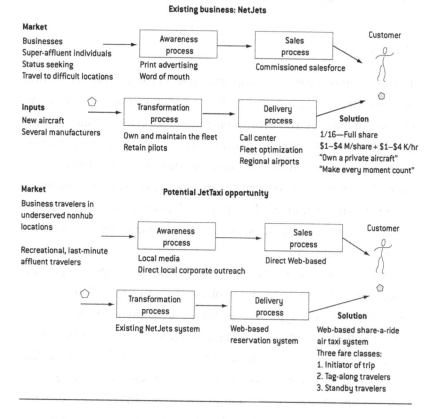

STRUCTURING THE FRONT END OF A TOURNAMENT

The previous section outlined techniques that can guide you and your employees in generating opportunities. In our experience, virtually anyone can generate some interesting opportunities by following these guidelines. Engage a group of people in the process for a day or so, and you'll obtain dozens, if not hundreds, of ideas. In doing so, you'll have mined the raw ore from which you can extract exceptional opportunities. But how do you organize your ideas into a tournament? We now describe two approaches to innovation tournaments: a hands-on innovation workshop and a Web-based submission and evaluation system. We have used both of these approaches and comment on their relative advantages and disadvantages in the following pages.

Innovation Workshop

To run an innovation workshop, assemble a group of twenty to forty participants. Participants will typically come from inside your organization, but might also include customers, suppliers, or industry experts. If the set of people you would like involved in your innovation workshop gets too large, you might organize several separate workshops. You should try to recruit as diverse a group of participants as possible; you're better off having people from a variety of departments than having one workshop for marketing employees and another for accountants.

At the beginning of the workshop, define the scope of opportunities that you're seeking and explain why you are looking for opportunities of this type. For example, you might explain to the participants that you are seeking opportunities that will help your brand be perceived as more environmentally friendly because this has emerged as a new customer requirement. Or you might explain that you are seeking opportunities to expand into China, because this is an important growth market. (See chapter 5 for more details about how to define the scope of a tournament.) Then, announce that the goal of the workshop is to identify a small set of exceptional opportunities.

For the workshop, equip participants with some or all of the idea-generation tools reviewed earlier in this chapter and allocate enough time. We have run workshops successfully in as little as an hour, but you may spend several hours over multiple sessions and weeks.

Start by asking people to spend ten to twenty minutes generating ideas on their own. Then bring folks together in groups of four to five. Each group will generate further opportunities and clarify and articulate the complete set of opportunities generated. To complete their work, the groups should summarize each opportunity on a single sheet paper or on a separate flip-chart page. (Chapter 4 explains how to organize, evaluate, and screen these opportunities in a workshop format.)

Web-Based Submission

An alternative to a workshop is online submission and evaluation. Along with this book, we've developed a Web-based software tool, called the Darwinator, to manage the early rounds of an innovation tournament. The Darwinator is available for use by readers of this book through our Web site www.InnovationTournaments.com. You can also use your own Web-based file-sharing system and survey tool.

We designed the Darwinator to allow any participant to submit opportunities comprising a title, description, and an image, if desired. The interface ensures anonymity, minimizing the effects of office politics. You give employees a deadline by which they must submit opportunities. We find that also setting a target of five to ten opportunities stimulates participation. The amount of time allowed for submissions can vary. We have often allowed one or two weeks. Just as for the workshop, chapter 4 discusses how to evaluate the opportunities submitted in this way.

HARNESSING THE CREATIVE ABILITIES OF INDIVIDUALS AND GROUPS

Some individuals seem to be naturally creative and enthusiastically generate opportunities. Others are more reluctant participants in the innovation process. Here are a few ways to get the most from your employees.

The Creative Few

You probably wouldn't be surprised to learn that different people in your organization have different levels of skill in singing or playing tennis. They probably also differ substantially in their ability to identify exceptional opportunities.

As part of our research, we studied opportunities identified by a group of forty-seven managers in the Wharton School's executive MBA program who were working together to create a new business. The executives had an average of ten years of work experience. We asked each one to identify about five unique business ideas and submit them via the Darwinator. Each participant also evaluated about one hundred opportunities submitted by his or her teammates, rating them on a scale of 1 to 10. The Darwinator then averaged the evaluations to produce an estimate of the quality of the opportunities.

Figure 2-6 is a histogram of the estimated quality of the opportunities generated by the group. The dark bars represent the opportunities generated by the top 25 percent of the group, based on the average quality of the opportunities they generated. You can see that the top few folks, as measured by the quality of their average ideas, generated most of the *best* ideas. (A formal statistical analysis of the data reveals that variation *across individuals* explains much of the variation in quality of the opportunities.[7]) We don't know whether these differences spring from differences in talent, effort, or application of tools.[8] Regardless, if dramatic differences in ability persist over time, then you should focus your energies on harnessing the efforts of your best innovators rather than on trying to squeeze ideas out of those who don't excel at the task (but who may have other skills).

Working in Groups

Business orthodoxy says that the best way to generate new ideas is to recruit a group and brainstorm. But dozens of studies have shown that if the objective is to generate lots of ideas, then people working independently will outperform those same folks working together.[9]

FIGURE 2-6

The quality distribution of opportunities generated by a group of forty-seven professionals and (in black) the opportunities that were generated by the top quarter of the group.

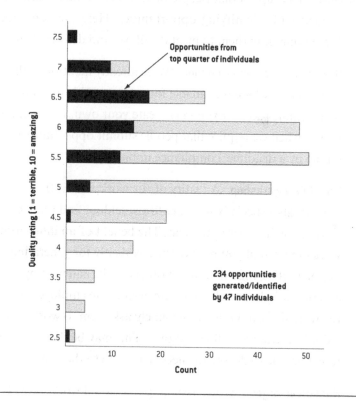

Our own research shows that, per unit of time invested, individuals are three to seven times more productive in generating ideas than are the same people in a group.

Why? In a conventional meeting people speak consecutively, and that becomes a bottleneck. Likewise, group dynamics may inhibit individuals from freely expressing their ideas: some people are shy; others are intimidated. But while the number of ideas generated by individuals working separately is substantially higher, our research also suggests that group sessions can produce more varied ideas, some very good and some very bad. With increased variation comes an increased chance to discover exceptional opportunities.[10]

Deadlines and Deliverables

A weakness of groups is that people often don't do their homework when charged with identifying opportunities. Here are some techniques for encouraging them to meet deadlines and deliver ideas.

- **Use an online submission tool.** We've already mentioned the Darwinator, which is available for your use. You may find other online tools, or you may create your own. In our experience, when we require that people submit opportunities online by a deadline, compliance improves.

- **Schedule a workshop.** A reality of the workplace is that individuals, especially in larger firms, seldom find time to work alone in generating ideas. The benefit of an innovation workshop is that you reserve time explicitly for generating opportunities, time that might otherwise be eaten up by e-mails and phone calls. You can even invite employees to the workshop and then immediately ask them to work individually during the allocated time. This may be the only way to get people to devote the necessary time to the task.

- **Numerical targets.** When assigning individual work, provide a specific target for the number of opportunities to be generated. The number will depend on the domain. If generating product or company names, you might pick fifty or one hundred, but for new business models, you might say three. Your targets can be used in multiple phases. We sometimes assign individuals to generate, say, ten opportunities for a first meeting. Then, we ask them to generate another ten for the next meeting. That's less daunting than requiring twenty from the start.

- **Templates.** To summarize ideas, we use a one-page template that includes graphically defined regions for a title, a sketch, and a description. When faced with a template, individuals tend to fill in the required elements. There is something about a form that prompts them to fill in the blanks. Templates not only seem to spur individuals and groups to be more assiduous in their thinking and preparation, but also to help standardize descriptions for comparison. A well-designed template can also make a fine display device for opportunities when posted on the walls of a meeting room.

SUMMARY

Organizations typically generate about half of their opportunities for innovation internally. Because opportunities are the key ingredients for successful innovation tournaments, improving your opportunity generation is critical.

This chapter presented several techniques to help you improve. Other tools are available from our Web site. As we discuss in the next chapter, you should complement your internally generated opportunities with ones from outside your firm. Remember, the more opportunities that compete in your tournament, the better the odds for an exceptional opportunity.

Opportunities are generated by human beings, not by machines. People are unpredictable and heterogeneous. Some are much better than others at generating opportunities. Try to identify your best players and invest in their efforts. Tools that facilitate idea generation include online submission, templates, and numerical targets.

Diagnostics

⇒ What fraction of the opportunities you consider is generated internally by members of your staff?

⇒ Have you identified the few individuals in your organization who are particularly good at generating opportunities?

➡ Have you trained your staff in techniques for generating opportunities?

➡ Do you and your employees regularly devote time and effort to generating opportunities?

➡ How do you structure the front end of the tournament process to capture opportunities generated internally?

➡ What templates and other administrative techniques do you apply to the opportunity generation process?

3

OUTSIDE SOURCES

Sensing Opportunities Externally

Innovators work inside big established firms like Microsoft, Pfizer, and Honda and in start-ups from Shanghai to Silicon Valley. Their efforts improve their firms' competitive prospects. But opportunities for innovation also bubble outside firms in places like university labs and hobbyists' garages. Thus, in addition to generating opportunities internally, innovative firms must also sense them externally.

Consider the success story of the energy drink Red Bull. The Austrian entrepreneur Dietrich Mateschitz created an impressive business with sales of 3.5 billion cans of the sweet, caffeinated drink in 2007 (not to mention two Formula 1 teams and a soccer club). But he didn't invent it. He found it. The original recipe was developed in Thailand by a company called TC Pharmaceutical and sold under the Thai name Krating Daeng. Truck drivers, construction workers, farmers, and other people who worked long hours liked to consume it to fight fatigue.[1]

Mateschitz worked in Thailand for a German toothpaste company. On one of his trips to the country, he tried Krating Daeng and found that it helped ease his jet lag. In 1987, he adapted the recipe to Austrian tastes by adding carbonation and cutting the sweetness. Sales soon took off. Mateschitz's company now competes with such beverage industry giants as Coca-Cola and PepsiCo.

Like Mateschitz, successful innovators need to scan their environment, sensing opportunities from customers, suppliers, competitors, universities, and companies in distant geographic regions. This chapter will help you do that by showing you how to understand when externally generated opportunities matter most and how to set up sensing mechanisms to help you identify them.

WHEN EXTERNAL INNOVATION IS MOST IMPORTANT

Innovation in the aircraft industry demands technical expertise, large development teams, and lots of money. Innovation in snack foods requires little more than a home kitchen. The *minimum required scale* for innovation helps to determine whether innovation should be done internally or, at least partly, externally.

A team of thousands of people at Boeing, for example, developed the 787 Dreamliner commercial airframe at a cost of billions of dollars.[2] Boeing can be confident that a couple of latter-day Wright brothers won't cobble together a competing plane in their garage. The Coca-Cola Company, in contrast, enjoys no such comfort. Competitors like Red Bull can pop up anywhere.

In some fields, innovation requires deep expertise but only modest amounts of money. Individual surgeons, for example, have created many orthopedic devices, including the Taylor Spatial Fixator. Recognition of the need required expertise, but creation of a solution called for only a modest investment in basic mechanical design and fabrication.

Many Web-based innovations also require industry-specific smarts but neither decades of experience nor scads of money. Witness YouTube, created by Chad Hurley, Steve Chen, and Jawed Karim, former PayPal employees. They devised their basic Web site, which plays videos over the Web, in a matter of months in early 2005 and sought venture capital only after launching it. In the world of the so-called Web 2.0, the biggest expenses for software entrepreneurs are typically rent, a handful of desktop computers, and plenty of late-night pizzas and Red Bull.

If you operate in a resource- and expertise-intensive industry like Boeing's (i.e., the minimum required scale is large in your industry), your firm is protected, to some extent, from guerilla innovators and garage hobbyists, and you can invest less in sensing and scanning activities. You can focus more on internal generation than on external sensing. But if you operate in a field like YouTube's, you must be sensitive to opportunities discovered and exploited by innovators outside the core group of established players.

Figure 3-1 illustrates two key dimensions associated with the resources required for innovation. Industries in which the minimum required scale of innovation is large are on the right of the chart. By and large, these industries are protected from guerilla innovators. If you find yourself located on the left, however, you need to be watchful. In the upper left corner of the chart, new opportunities are most likely to be produced by a highly skilled professional, potentially working for a research lab or a university. In the lower left corner, you might find your next competitor operating in a small bar or a home kitchen right now.

WHERE TO SENSE EXTERNALLY

Sensing opportunities externally requires that you scan the world around you. You can't wait until opportunities come to you. In this section, we discuss ways you can do this. Often, after you've identified external opportunities, you follow up with the internal generation of alternatives. Again, consider Red Bull. Mateschitz sensed the initial opportunity externally. But he also adapted it to the local

FIGURE 3-1

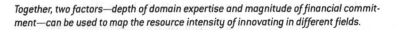

Together, two factors—depth of domain expertise and magnitude of financial commitment—can be used to map the resource intensity of innovating in different fields.

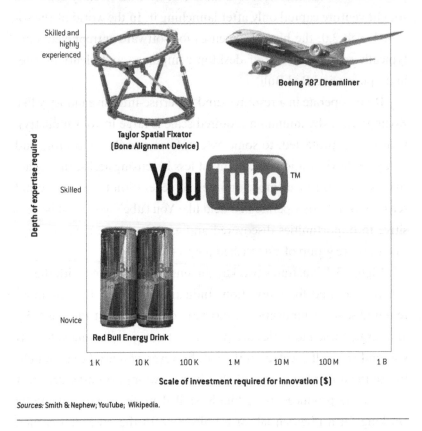

Sources: Smith & Nephew; YouTube; Wikipedia.

tastes of the Austrian market—a process that probably included substantial internal generation efforts.

The following pages describe a set of techniques that help you create new opportunities by sensing innovation activities outside your organization.

Import Geographically Isolated Innovations

Innovations are often geographically isolated, particularly if introduced by smaller firms. Translating the innovation from one geographic region to another can be a source of innovation. Again, re-call the Red Bull story. What started as a product for Thai cab driv-ers became the drink for New York investment bankers and Silicon Valley tech geeks. This example is by no means unique. Witness Star-bucks. Founder Howard Schultz created the chain after visiting Milan and becoming infatuated with its café culture and espresso-based drink concoctions.

You can sense opportunities by identifying outstanding products or services in a distant region and then considering how you might adapt them to a different place. For example, what about the face masks worn in Japan to prevent the spread of viruses? What about the auto-mated bicycle rental systems deployed widely in Oslo and Paris?

Identify Small Companies with Niche Products That Have the Potential for Broader Market Appeal

Small companies can thrive in the ecological niches ignored by large companies. These niches can support the development of an oppor-tunity to the point at which much of the risk and uncertainty has been resolved. On occasion, an innovation made in a niche will be suitable for a much larger market.

For example, a small company in California called Gyration de-veloped a hand-motion sensor technology for television remote con-trols. The gaming company Nintendo sought out and acquired this technology for use in the Wii video game remote control, an applica-tion with an enormously larger market than the niche market originally addressed by Gyration (figure 3-2). The Wii became an enormous suc-cess and sold more than 20 million units by the end of 2007.[3]

Cherry-Pick from a Full-Line Company

Larger companies tend to grow in part by gradually adding products. As a result, many of them have hefty product lines and knotty supply chains and need complex production systems to support them. If a competitor produces only one product, but in the richest part of the

FIGURE 3-2

The remote control for the Wii gaming system by Nintendo embodies a technology originally developed for a niche application by a small company, Gyration.

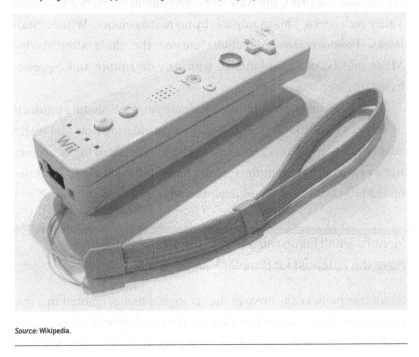

Source: Wikipedia.

market, it can often do so at dramatically lower cost. The product can often be sourced from a third party, reducing fixed costs, and then priced attractively. The established firm may be hamstrung in its ability to respond because of a reluctance to abandon its full-line strategy. Think of this as the guerilla approach: you find a diversified and preferably complacent company and then offer its highest-margin product or service at a better price.

Identify Lead Users and Study Their Innovation Activities

Firms have ample incentive to innovate. Innovation, after all, can result in new sources of cash. But lead users and independent inventors may have even greater incentives. Lead users are people or firms that have advanced needs for products or services that are not being met by other companies.[4] They must either tolerate their unmet needs or innovate themselves to address them. Take Dr. Lillian Aronson, a veterinarian at the University of Pennsylvania who performs feline kidney transplants. Her procedure is relatively new, the market is small, and few existing surgical tools fit the task. Dr. Aronson thus has to choose between ill-suited instruments and inventing her own. If she invents a useful device, she creates an opportunity for further innovation by an established firm.

Listen to Independent Inventors (And Let Them Shoulder the Risk of Failure)

Independent inventors likewise create new solutions. Their motives differ—and often defy the simple calculus of dollars and cents. Research by Åstebro on about two thousand inventions by independent inventors found that a majority of their inventions lost money and that, even looking across all inventions as a group, inventors lose money on average.[5] Why would people pour time into something with such poor returns?

They could be hobbyists, wild optimists, or even "lottery players," attracted to mathematically unfair games that provide a very small chance of an enormous return. Regardless of their motives, independent inventors do toil in many fields. Most of their efforts don't result in successful innovation, but a tiny fraction of inventors do manage to identify a match between an unmet need and a new solution. These matches may provide opportunities for existing firms through licensing or acquisition.[6]

One way you can identify independent inventors is by participating in online communities. For example, we found the opportunity SpoilMySpouse (see figure I-1) at the Web-based innovation network Cambrian House (www.cambrianhouse.com). This site, and several others, are used by independent inventors to present, discuss, and refine the opportunities on which they work.

Cooperate with Universities

The first large-scale digital computer was invented at the University of Pennsylvania, four blocks from where we wrote this book. Today Penn is the source of many commercial innovations in medicine and other fields. Major research universities are wellsprings of opportunities and have produced such successes as Google (Stanford), Genzyme (MIT), and many others.[7] Some of the opportunities spring from faculty-led research, particularly in the life sciences. Others are created by the legions of bright young students who enroll to chart new directions in their lives and careers. Engaging with universities usually requires a multifaceted approach. You can recruit on-campus for interns and employees, sponsor new product-design and business-plan competitions, join research consortia, and participate in campus conferences and events.

CREATING MECHANISMS FOR SENSING OPPORTUNITIES EXTERNALLY

Viktor Gordeyev, a Russian aircraft engineer, wanted to run and jump without tiring, so he conceived a way to marry running shoes with tiny gas-powered engines and pogo stick–like pistons. His invention, which resembles stilts more than shoes, enables a runner to move at 22 miles per hour (figure 3-3). But the Russian army claimed the shoes, and they languished as a classified secret for years. After they were declassified in the mid-1990s, an entrepreneur tried to commercialize them, but they never caught on.[8]

Granted, gas-powered shoes have their drawbacks—the engines can misfire, throwing a runner off balance—but they're just the kind of extreme opportunity that should be detected by innovators working in the field of transportation. Recall our argument from the introduction: your number of exceptional opportunities can be increased by (1) increasing the average quality of your opportunities, (2) increasing the number of them, and (3) increasing the variance in their

FIGURE 3-3

Boots powered by internal combustion and created by an independent inventor, Russian engine designer Viktor Gordeyev.

Source: Joseph Sywenky/Redux.

quality. If gas-powered shoes aren't a "high variance" idea, then what is?

And thus we shift to the task of *sensing*, that is, finding novel ideas such as Gordeyev's piston-powered shoes. In particular, we suggest four ways of sensing opportunities externally: passive reception, active scanning, social networking, and innovation contests.

Passive Reception of Opportunities

If you operate in a field where thousands of talented people vie for attention, you might simply announce your needs and await the flood of submissions. First Round Capital, for example, is an early-stage venture fund with a stellar reputation among entrepreneurs, as reflected in a top rating on the popular Web site TheFunded.com. As a result, the firm sees dozens of unsolicited business plans every week. (However, even popular venture capitalists will say that although they look at every plan that they receive passively, they also have to work actively to solicit the best opportunities.) A few other fields are buyers' markets, including the movie and music businesses and professional athletics. If you don't work in one of these fields, you may still benefit from soliciting submissions from outsiders but can't rely on it as your only source of opportunities.

Active Scanning of Communication Channels

Journalists, bloggers, and conference organizers are in the business of sensing. Although their insights are available to everyone, you cannot ignore the opportunities that they reveal. Several members of your organization should therefore actively scan the channels that are relevant to your business. Table 3-1 lists a few of the communication channels useful in identifying opportunities for innovation in consumer products and services enabled by the Internet. Of course, cardiology will have very different channels, including some listed in table 3-2.

Representation in Social Networks

Another way to increase the keenness of your sensing is to ensure that your firm hires and retains people who are connected to the right

TABLE 3-1

Examples of communication channels useful in identifying opportunities in Internet services.

Print media	Web-based media	Events
New York Times	Technorati.com	TED
Wall Street Journal	SocialComputingMagazine.com	Consumer Electronics Show
Wired	Lifehacker.com	
BusinessWeek	Knowledge@Wharton	
Fortune		
Inc.		

TABLE 3-2

Examples of communication channels useful in identifying opportunities in cardiology.

Print media	Web-based media	Events
New England Journal of Medicine	Acc.org	ACC Annual Scientific Session
Circulation	Cardiosource.com	ACC i2 Summit
Journal of the American College of Cardiology	Medbioworld.com	
European Heart Journal		
Science		
Nature		

social networks. Consider the network of inventors depicted in figure 3-4. Two gatekeepers link the otherwise tightly clustered groups of inventors. In this network, one would prefer to employ one of the two engineers at the key nodes in the network, rather than those on the periphery. Individuals at the key nodes link several clusters and provide efficient access to opportunities arising throughout the network.[9]

Social institutions of all kinds facilitate communication among innovators. Some of these institutions may not be related to professional life. Cricket and softball leagues in Silicon Valley are widely known to be hotbeds of entrepreneurial activity and have played a key role in facilitating the exchange of ideas leading to opportunities for new ventures.

Innovation Contests

Still another approach to sensing opportunities can be found in innovation contests. In an innovation contest, individuals or teams submit plans or prototypes, which are typically judged by experts, sometimes with the help of panels of users. The evaluators rank the raw ideas or sometimes early prototypes.

TV retailer QVC's product road show uses this approach. It visits ten cities in the United States annually to screen new products. Staples, the office-supplies retailer, likewise encourages consumers to submit product proposals. In return, the creators receive royalties if the company introduces their ideas. It's a double win. Staples gets

FIGURE 3-4

A network of inventors in Silicon Valley circa 1990. Two individuals form key nodes in the network, linking otherwise separate organizations.

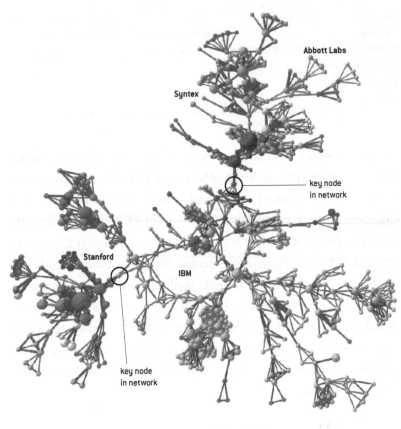

Source: Adapted from an image by L. Fleming and I. Baker, Harvard Business School.

inexpensive ideas, while its most creative customers earn extra money. Figure 3-5 shows three products that the company launched in this way.

Even the U.S. government uses innovation contests. The U.S. Defense Advanced Research Projects Agency (DARPA) entices inventors to enter its Grand Challenge for autonomous robotic vehicles (ARVs), which have explored the surface of Mars, among other uses, by offering prize money. The winner of the DARPA's 2006

FIGURE 3-5

Staples obtained these products by relying on the external creation of opportunities: Wordlock (left), Strap Stapler (center), and Rubber Bandits (right).

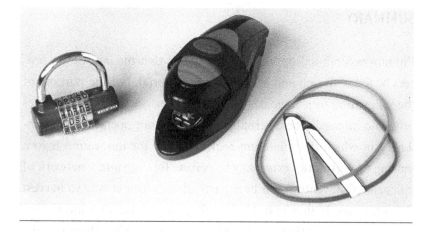

Grand Challenge received $2 million. DARPA, for its part, obtains ideas for ARV innovations that would be hard to develop internally.

This sort of competition can quickly and inexpensively create a broad range of ideas from a diverse set of inventors. The ideas then can be refined by professional development teams and tested with traditional market research. Contests also often manage to tap into inventors' nonfinancial motives, such as the bragging rights that come with winning and seeing an invention turned into a commercial product. Few people can claim that their idea has made it onto the surface of Mars. What's more, contest participants, often lacking financial backing and easy access to capital markets, typically couldn't handsomely benefit from their innovations if they kept them to themselves.

The company Innocentive specializes in organizing innovation contests for a wide range of business settings. It allows corporations, government agencies, and nonprofit organizations to publish a problem related to research and development to a large community of innovators around the world. The best solutions are then rewarded with prize money ranging from $5,000 to $1,000,000. Whether the problem is to find a new catalyst for a chemical reaction or a new product concept, this form of innovation contest provides a diverse set of new opportunities.

SUMMARY

Finding exceptional opportunities requires that the innovation process be fed with rich and abundant raw material. For the purpose of the innovation tournament, it doesn't matter whether opportunities originate internally or externally. But if you are operating in an industry in which the minimum required scale for innovation is low, sensing opportunities externally is a must. Tapping into a network of independent inventors can be a particularly efficient way to harvest opportunities. If they're hobbyists, they may chase after mostly impractical ideas, but that won't matter to them. They're often pursuing a passion, not payoff.

External opportunities can be found in many other places, too, including in faraway and niche markets, full-line companies with complex product lines, lead users, and universities. Avail yourself of all of them.

The timing of your sensing matters. Sensing the opportunity when it appears on the front page of the *Wall Street Journal* is easy; sensing it while being driven in a cab in Thailand is not. Thus, sensing is most beneficial when the signal that you are sensing is still weak. And for that, you have to listen very carefully.

This chapter discussed several mechanisms that facilitate the sensing of external opportunities at times when the opportunities are still at an embryonic stage and the corresponding signals are weak: passive receipt of opportunities, active scanning of communication channels, participation in social networks, and innovation contests. All these efforts lead to the identification of additional opportunities that are added to the list of internally generated opportunities that you obtained from your internal generation efforts. The contestants are now assembled. It is time for the first round of elimination.

Diagnostics

⟹ What are the relative ratios of the sources of opportunities? Do a lot of opportunities come from customers, competitive products, partners, independent inventors, distribution partners, and from structured exploration within the firm?

⟹ What is the minimum scale of resources for innovating in your industry? How much specialized expertise is required? Where, therefore, are opportunities likely to come from?

⟹ What are the information channels containing opportunities relative to your business? Who is scanning them?

⟹ What small companies are active in your field? Do you have contacts and relationships with them?

⟹ Do you have a policy and mechanism for receiving submissions from external innovators?

⟹ Have you considered running an innovation contest to stimulate the creation of opportunities outside your company?

ELIMINATION ROUND

Screening Opportunities

In anticipation of the 2012 Olympic Games in London, the United Kingdom, as the host, is dreaming of gold, silver, and bronze. In recent games, the country was among the top ten medal winners, but it wants more. So in 2006, the British Olympic Association announced a campaign to improve the country's medal count. Its 20-4-2012 initiative, standing for twenty gold medals and a fourth place in the overall count, aims to evaluate 1.5 million British children, ages eleven through sixteen (in 2006), and recruit those with the most athletic potential into Olympic sports like judo, badminton, and rowing.[1]

In a first round of selection, evaluators will compare the physiological data of each of the kids to a set of profiles that capture the ideal characteristics for athletes in all Olympic sports. Basketball players, for example, are typically long-armed and tall, whereas rowers need strong hearts and lungs. The 100,000 most promising candidates will be invited to enter the second round of evaluations, which will consist of full days packed with various sport-specific diagnostics. That group will be winnowed to 1,000, who will then start training with the specialized coaches.

The British medal push shares a critical quality with corporate innovation: a particular individual can apply only the sweat and toil of daily hard work to increase his or her chances of winning gold, but a nation, like a company, has a much more powerful lever, namely *selection*. A well-designed selection process will prevent a country from wasting its limited resources trying to turn wisps into weightlifters. And it will do so efficiently.

Opportunity screening, the subject of this chapter, is the first step in the selection process that aims to identify exceptional opportunities from the pool of opportunities you have collected. It's the qualification phase of the innovation tournament.

What makes for a good screening process? Whether it is British measurements of athleticism or a company's selection of innovation opportunities, an effective process must fulfill two requirements:

1. Given the number of opportunities to be screened, it must be *efficient*. It must be cheap and fast, favoring quick judgments based on imperfect information over lengthy discussion and extensive data collection.

2. It must be *accurate* despite the uncertainty that still clouds the prospects for a particular opportunity.

These two requirements, efficiency and accuracy, are in tension with each other. On the one hand, given the amount of work associated with in-depth review, you'd prefer to focus on the most promising opportunities. On the other, you want to examine all opportunities in detail so that you don't kill the wrong ones.

The best way you can overcome this tension is by evaluating opportunities in multiple rounds. From round to round, you narrow the field of opportunities. That enables you to more carefully assess the remaining ones. In the first rounds of screening, your filtering stresses efficiency. As the opportunities reach the later stages, you shift the emphasis to accuracy. This is the structure of the innovation tournament we outlined in the introduction.

Let's revisit the U.K. Olympics example to see how you might apply this thinking. A computer could screen the young athletes' physiological profiles, saving the time of coaches and kids. Coaches or trainers would have to perform the second-round evaluations, which only need to take a day each. That would let the British program devote its resources to the third round, the comprehensive training of top candidates. Opportunity screening resembles a director's casting for a movie, a consulting firm's recruitment of new trainees, or the tryouts for professional sports teams.

The logic behind the innovation tournament is summarized in figure 4-1. Opportunities enter on the left of the figure (see chapters 2 and 3) and move through several rounds of screening. The best ideas move forward for an in-depth analysis, described in coming chapters. Many books on innovation and R&D management refer to variants of this figure as the "innovation funnel." The funnel metaphor doesn't quite work. In a funnel, whatever enters also leaves. Good screening eliminates many opportunities, preventing the bad ideas from leaving. It's more of a filter than a funnel.

In this chapter, we outline three rounds of filtering. In the first round, we emphasize efficiency, explaining how to collect and vote on opportunities using a Web-based system. In the second round, we balance efficiency and accuracy, showing you how to run an innovation workshop. And in the third round, we shift the emphasis to accuracy. At this point, you'll evaluate each opportunity comprehensively, measuring feasibility and financial attractiveness.

To get a sense of what screening must accomplish, examine table 4-1. It shows a fraction of the 234 opportunities that were created as discussed in chapter 2. Faced with a long list like this, filtering must focus on efficiency. Otherwise, you'll waste time. Plus, creating opportunities is cheap, so a smart company will generate lots of them,

FIGURE 4-1

The screening phase of an innovation tournament has to be able to handle a large number of raw opportunities. Screening is often done in multiple rounds, with increasing sophistication in the selection methods that are applied.

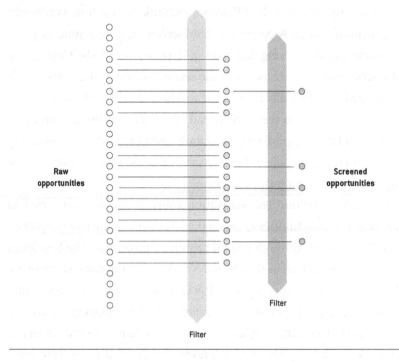

knowing that that gives it a greater likelihood of finding an exceptional one.

EFFICIENCY-DRIVEN SCREENING OF OPPORTUNITIES: THE DARWINATOR

As we discussed in chapter 2, you can ask employees to submit their ideas using a Web-based system; ours is called the Darwinator and is available for your use at www.InnovationTournaments.com. A Web-based interface ensures that participants do not know the author of each idea, so they will base their vote on the quality of the opportu-

TABLE 4-1

An example list of opportunities faced by a team contemplating a new venture. Each opportunity includes a text description (not shown).

Online service professional rating	Executive compensation index ("ECI")
Peer-to-peer gaming	The ultimate travel assistant
Smart parking meter	Heated ski poles
"GeriAthletes"—exercise facilities for those over the hill	Cell phone detector for retail businesses
Fuel price hedging Web site	Fuel price guru
"SureTemp"—programmable temperature faucet	Airport haven
Pooled purchasing marketplace	Keeping track of your shopping lists online
Chaat—Indian snack house	College-level programs over the radio
Coaching for coaches	Internet TV guide
Sports ticket timeshare	Groceries drive-thru
Home energy consultants	Complain-o-rama
Total health—holistic meets classic medicine	CharmBus—portable beauty consultants
Outsourcing agency for small companies	Marketing communications consulting
Life planning simulator	HandyMan valet
NannyOnCall	Business school identifier
Kid service Web site—"ParentsHelp"	Airplane dating
Fill my iPod (Cause I don't have time to do it myself!)	Lux linens
Cell-phone door/garage-door opener	Healthy coffee
Childcare on demand	Disposable car cover
Virtual executive assistants	Indian mall restaurants
Low-carb ice cream in India	Resealable flexible packaging for cereal
Wireless headphones for multiple listeners	IntelliAds—we know who you are
Vacation designer	SMS daily local weather update service
Online e-books for textbooks	Car consultants
Tandem umbrella stroller	ARiddleADay
Web site to fit PDA display screen	HandyMan valet, painting service
Education supersite	Online airport guide
Voice-activated car controls	Fido for a day
Diversity recruiting	Star sightings
Service bartering	Global impact calculator
Gift advisor	Cell phone over the radio

nity, not their opinion of its inventor. If you give people several weeks for their submissions, you're likely to receive hundreds of them. Figure 4-2 summarizes the flow of Web-based innovation tournaments, showing the submission of opportunities on the left, followed by evaluation. That leads to selection of the best.

FIGURE 4-2

Along with this book, we developed a software tool, the Darwinator, that we have found to be powerful in its support of opportunity screening. Available through the book's Web site, it supports the submission of opportunities, the rating process, and the statistical analysis of votes.

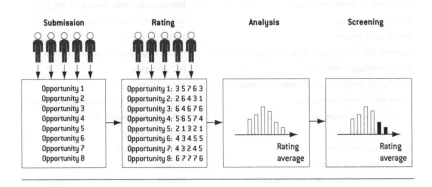

After all opportunities have been submitted, participants rate the opportunities. You'll accomplish your first-round goal of efficiency in two ways:

- Each opportunity is summarized on one Web page, so it typically takes less than a minute to rate it, typically on a scale of 1 (poor) to 10 (excellent).

- The Darwinator allows you to control the number of participants voting on an opportunity and ensures that the same number of evaluators, usually ten to twenty, sees each one.

We used the Darwinator to review the 234 opportunities mentioned earlier and had each opportunity evaluated by twenty people; thus, we gathered thousands of ratings. The automation of the clerical tasks makes this easy. Based on the voting, you decide which opportunities to move to the next round of the innovation tournament. Typically, you'd advance ones with high average ratings or high variance in their ratings, that is, ones that some raters love but others hate. Opportunities that polarize raters are high-variance opportunities, and recall that in an innovation tournament variance is a desirable property.

As you can see in figure 4-3, the bell-shaped curve, which captures the various levels of quality across opportunities that we have alluded to earlier in this book, is not just an academic thought experiment. We have run numerous innovation tournaments (four of which are displayed in the figure) and consistently observed a bell-shaped distribution of quality. Thus, although the quality of each individual opportunity is random, the overall outcome of the quality distribution that results from the opportunity generation process is predictable.

FIGURE 4-3

The outcome of the rating process is a quality score for each opportunity, which can be used to create a histogram of the set of opportunities. The vertical axis is a Z score—how much better or worse an opportunity is than average, expressed in units of the distribution's standard deviation. [See Web site for statistical details.]

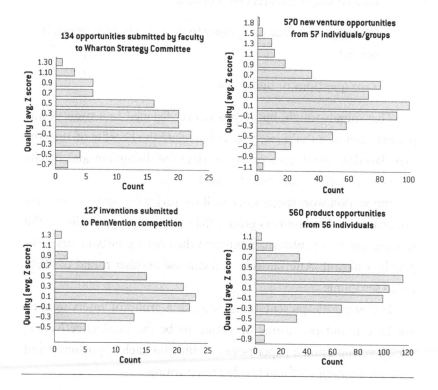

BALANCING EFFICIENCY AND ACCURACY: THE INNOVATION WORKSHOP

In chapter 2, we talked about how you could use innovation workshops to generate ideas. You can also use the workshop to evaluate opportunities. Often, you'll ask creators to pitch their ideas to a group and support their presentation with a PowerPoint slide or poster. Oral presentations take up more time than Web-based screening does, but they can yield greater accuracy because each opportunity is explained in greater detail and is typically evaluated by more people.

At this point, the pool of potential opportunities typically remains large, often fifty or more, so presentations should adhere strictly to the "2-1-0 rule":

➡ Two minutes of presentation by an individual, with a bell used to keep presenters on schedule

➡ One page of a slide or a poster to provide visual support, if needed

➡ Zero questions or discussion

This sounds tough, but if you've ever listened to a twenty-slide presentation of a dud idea, you'll appreciate the benefits of this format. Besides, you'll have plenty of time for discussion and debate once you've further narrowed the field.

Innovation workshops work well for reviewing up to about fifty opportunities. For numbers greater than fifty, we suggest splitting the tournament into subtournaments and then having the winners compete in a playoff. Alternatively, you can use another round of Web-based screening.

Following the presentations, you ask a group of raters to vote. We have found two forms of voting to be the most effective: (1) sticker voting using a paper poster or slide for each opportunity and a sticker for each vote and (2) electronic voting.

With sticker voting, you display opportunities on flip-chart sheets or letter-sized printouts posted on the walls of the room where you're conducting your workshop. Each opportunity should be summarized in one page, and voters should have had a chance to acquaint themselves with all of the ideas before the meeting. At the meeting, they're given dots (or other types of stickers) to register their votes. They simply apply their stickers to the opportunities they favor.

There's no right answer with respect to how many opportunities each participant should be allowed to endorse. One rule of thumb is that the average number of votes per opportunity should be about five. So, for example, with fifty opportunities you would give out 250 dots. If there were twenty-five participants, each would therefore get 10 dots.[2] You can restrict your raters to only allotting one vote per opportunity or you can let them vote multiple times for a single one. If you allow an individual to vote more than once for an opportunity, you're giving passion a greater role in your deliberations.

How many raters should you use? Recall that you're aiming to quickly weed out the bottom half of the opportunities. Tough decisions loom in the near future, so you shouldn't waste your colleagues' time aiming for perfection here. More important than the number of participants is their diversity; they should represent different parts of your organization. Having said this, groups of ten to twenty raters are common.

A pitfall of sticker voting is that some people will wait to vote while watching what their colleagues do and then be influenced by the earlier votes. You can stem this conduct by allowing for a "shopping period" in which people ponder their votes but don't express them. If you number each opportunity, participants can write the number of an opportunity on each of their stickers during the decision period. In theory, everyone can then place their stickers more or less simultaneously.

Electronic voting can also head off the herd mentality. Several software vendors offer electronic voting tools.[3] Using such voting tools, you'd follow each pitch with an immediate vote. This approach works well if the voting is based primarily on oral presentations as opposed to posters or slides summarizing the opportunities.

Electronic voting also gives you a data set that you can analyze for patterns, such as "Our European sales organization prefers this opportunity" or "This one polarizes people—they love it or hate it." And it provides summary statistics beyond average ratings, such as the number of raters who assigned the highest possible score to the opportunity or the variance of the ratings.

Regardless of which voting method you choose, we suggest that you consider doing the following when organizing an innovation workshop:

➡ **Examine distributions.** You might want to advance an opportunity that did not stand out based on its average rating, yet had several very enthusiastic supporters. Strong opinions often point to exceptional ideas.

➡ **Identify hotspots.** Categorize opportunities by identifying clusters of related opportunities, sometimes called hotspots.[4] Hotspots reveal what the opportunity creators focused on and can anticipate problems that may arise during voting: if, say, five opportunities are almost identical, yet are presented as different, none might receive many votes and thus all of them could be eliminated. But if you combined opportunities in a hotspot, the underlying idea could get enough votes to survive.

EMPHASIZING ACCURACY: SCREENING BASED ON CRITERIA

Workshops with voting are fun and balance efficiency and accuracy. But as you reach the later rounds of your innovation tournament, you should complement subjective decision making based on incomplete information with objective criteria and data, as we do with the examples that follow. One employs a subjective evaluation along a set of predefined criteria; the other uses a checklist of general business criteria.

First consider table 4-2, which shows a set of chemical compounds under consideration for further development at Merck.[5] Merck has ranked each compound on a scale of 1 to 5, with 5 being the highest score, on four criteria: potency, safety, strategic fit, and financial return. When creating a table such as this one, you should, if possible, create objective guidelines for what constitutes, say, a score of 5 for safety. This score, for example, might correspond to specific chemical and medical properties.

If a set of opportunities doesn't lend itself to objective scoring, consider using experts, operating independently of each other, to assess the opportunities with respect to each of your criteria. You would then compare their scores. Again, consider Merck's situation. If all of the experts scored drug candidate Y (a diabetes treatment) as a 2 for potency, no further discussion would be needed at this stage. If, however, they disagreed about its potency, the group could discuss this particular attribute. Instead of wrestling with the daunting question "Which opportunities should we pursue?" the agenda item for a meeting would simply be "Potency evaluation for Y." A more focused question can yield more specific answers, and your experts can better determine precisely what information they'd need to resolve the uncertainty.

A second example is the *Real-Win-Worth-it* (RWW) criteria, developed by 3M. The name of the criteria summarizes the three questions the organization attempts to answer when screening opportunities:[6]

⇒ Is the opportunity *real*; that is, is there a real market that you can serve with the product or service? Criteria here include market size, potential pricing, availability of technology, and the ability to produce and deliver the product or service at high volume.

⇒ Can you *win* with this opportunity; that is, can you establish a sustainable competitive advantage? Can you patent or brand the idea? Are you more capable of executing it than competitors (for example, do you have superior engineering talent in this field)?

TABLE 4-2

Thirty compounds that Merck considered for preclinical development. Each of the compounds is scored on four criteria: potency, safety, strategic fit, and financial return. Data are partly disguised to protect confidential information.

Compound	Indication	Potency and selectivity (1–5 scale)	Safety (1–5 scale)	Strategic fit (1–5 scale)	Potential financial return (1–5 scale)
A	Respiratory 1	3	3	2	2
B	Respiratory 1	2	2	2	2
C	Respiratory 2	2	4	2	2
D	Obesity 1	3	2	4	4
E	Obesity 1	2	2	4	4
F	Obesity 2	2	2	4	5
G	Obesity 2	1	2	4	5
H	Depression 1	3	2	2	4
I	Depression 1	3	2	2	4
J	Metabolic disorder 1	4	2	2	4
K	Metabolic disorder 1	2	4	2	4
L	Cardiac 1	4	1	1	1
M	Cardiac 1	3	2	1	1
N	Cardiac 2	2	4	1	2
O	Alzheimer's 1	2	2	4	2
P	Alzheimer's 1	2	2	4	2
Q	Parkinson's 1	2	3	2	4
R	Osteoporosis 1	3	3	3	1
S	Osteoporosis 1	2	3	3	1
T	Pain 1	4	3	3	2
U	Pain 1	3	3	3	2
V	Pain 2	3	3	3	4
W	AIDS 1	3	1	1	2
X	AIDS 1	2	2	1	2
Y	Diabetes 1	2	4	4	4
Z	Diabetes 1	2	3	4	4
AA	Diabetes 1	1	3	4	4
BB	Diabetes 1	2	4	4	4
CC	Diabetes 2	2	3	4	5
DD	Diabetes 2	3	2	4	5

➡ Is the opportunity *worth it* financially? Do you have the resources needed (financial and developmental) and are you confident that the investment will be rewarded with appropriate returns?

Table 4-3 applies these criteria to the opportunity SpoilMySpouse discussed in the introduction from the hypothetical perspective of Google. The Excel checklist with the criteria is available at our book's Web site.

Besides their accuracy, another advantage of the RWW criteria is the ease with which you can communicate them to the people, whether staffers or outsiders, who are generating your opportunities. You're thus more likely to receive submissions that precisely meet your needs. Understand, however, that the RWW criteria will tend to align your creation of new opportunities with your current business needs and are thus biased in favor of incremental innovations. By their very nature, radical innovations lie outside of the limits that the RWW questions impose.

PRACTICAL ADVICE ON ORGANIZING EARLY-STAGE INNOVATION TOURNAMENTS

Based on our experience running dozens of early-stage innovation tournaments, we have compiled a few guidelines that may be helpful in addressing common pitfalls.

Sort Opportunities into Strategic Buckets

Opportunities not only vary widely in quality but also vary in the extent to which they support your firm's strategic direction. Some aim toward the development of new markets, whereas others enable the development of new capabilities or technologies. Conventional wisdom

TABLE 4-3

The Real-Win-Worth-it *criteria applied to the opportunity SpoilMySpouse discussed in the introduction from the hypothetical perspective of Google. The Excel checklist is available from this book's Web site.*

1. Is there a real market and a real product?		Notes
Is there a need? (What is the need? How is the need presently satisfied?)	Yes	
Can the customer buy? (Size of the market, customer decision-making process)	Yes	
Will the customer buy? (Perceived risks and benefits, expectations on price and availability)	Yes	Not clear if customer would pay.
Is there a real product concept? (Line extension vs. new to the world)	Yes	
Is the product acceptable within the social, legal, and environmental norms?	Yes	
Is the concept feasible? Can it be made? Is the technology available? Does it satisfy the needs?	Yes	
Will our product satisfy the market? Is there a relative advantage over other products?	Yes	Can be linked with other personalized Google products.
Can it be produced at low cost?	Yes	
Are the risks perceived by the customer acceptable? What are the barriers to adoption?	Yes	
Net	Yes	

2. Can we win? Can our product or service be competitive? Can we succeed as a company?		
Do we have a competitive advantage? Is it sustainable? (Performance, patents, barriers to entry, substitution, price)	Yes	
Is the timing right?	Yes	
Does it fit our brand?	Yes	
Will we beat our competition? (How much will they improve? Price trajectories, entrants)	Maybe	AOL and Yahoo have easier access to the consumer wallet.
Do we have superior resources? (Engineering, finance, marketing, production; fit with core competencies)	Yes	
Do we have the management that can win? (Experience? Fit with culture? Commitment to this opportunity?)	Maybe	Little experience with subscription services. Advertising model better.
Do we know the market as well or better than our competitors? (Customer behavior? Channels?)	Maybe	Some insights on the consumer's willingness to pay are missing.
Net	Probably	

3. Is it worth doing? Is the return adequate and the risk acceptable?		
Will it make money? (NPV)	Yes	If tied to an advertising model.
Do we have the resources and the cash to do this?	Yes	
Are the risks acceptable to us? (What could go wrong? Technical risk vs. market risk)	Yes	
Does it fit our strategy? (Fit with our growth expectation, impact on brand, embedded options)	Yes	
Net	Yes	

in innovation strategy says that companies should balance the *exploitation* of existing opportunities with the *exploration* of new ones. People also talk about *core* versus *peripheral* innovation or *incremental* versus *radical* innovation; these terms mean the same thing, and the distinctions can all be unified under the single perspective of *uncertainty horizons*.

Most innovations face two types of uncertainty:[7]

➡ **Technological uncertainty** describes your ability to execute the opportunity as planned. If the opportunity is based on a technology or capability that you have, the level of technological uncertainty is low. It's medium if the technology exists outside your firm, and large if the opportunity is based on new discoveries or advances.

➡ **Market uncertainty** describes your ability to understand and address the needs of a group of customers. For opportunities that address your existing customers, market uncertainty is low. It's medium for market segments adjacent to your current business but addressed by other firms, and large for markets that are not served by anyone.

These two dimensions are summarized by figure 4-4.[8]

The two dimensions of technological and market knowledge and uncertainty together dictate an opportunity's riskiness. We use the terms *horizon 1*, *horizon 2*, and *horizon 3* to characterize the aggregate risk that a firm faces in pursuing an opportunity.[9] The horizon analogy relates both to the time typically required to exploit an opportunity and the availability of the relevant know-how.

Especially if you have not explicitly limited the scope of your innovation tournament, chances are that you now face opportunities that are located all over the chart shown in figure 4-4. Faced with such a mix of opportunities representing differing levels of novelty in technology and or markets, it often can be difficult to run one big innovation tournament with all innovation opportunities. There are two reasons for this:

FIGURE 4-4

Depending on the amount of their uncertainty, we classify opportunities into three horizons, ranging from horizon 1 (low uncertainty) to horizon 3 (high uncertainty). The lower left part of the graph corresponds to an area of low uncertainty: opportunities here address familiar markets and use familiar technologies. Moving to the upper right increases risk substantially.

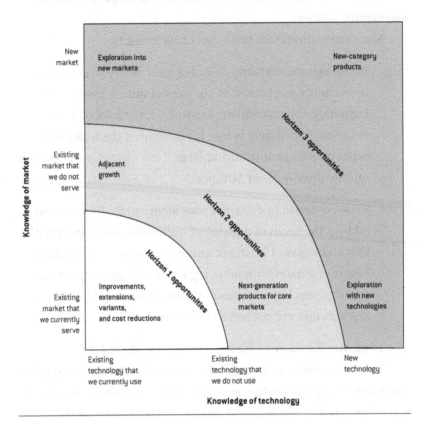

➡ It is difficult to compare two opportunities with each other if one aims to launch a global satellite network for mobile communications while the other one aims at adding two new colors to existing cell phone models.

➡ At the end of the screening process, we might have a large number of opportunities exploring new markets with existing technologies, yet we have not considered any opportunities that would use new technologies in our existing markets.

Given this kind of dilemma, you might want to run three separate innovation tournaments: one for horizon 1 opportunities, one for horizon 2, and one for horizon 3. Or you might consider running nine separate tournaments, each one corresponding to a combination of technological novelty (existing technology; new-to-the-firm technology; new-to-the-world technology) and market novelty (existing market that you serve; existing market that you don't serve; new market). Sorting the opportunities into separate horizons is often referred to as the *strategic bucket method.*[10]

You can define the scope of the tournaments before or after generating the opportunities. If you do so before opportunity generation, you can direct the creative efforts of the participants so that you achieve a balanced set of opportunities across strategic initiatives. If you wait to define the scope until after generating the opportunities, you might leave some important initiatives unsupported. However, you might also be surprised by exceptional opportunities that wouldn't have been created if you'd hewed to a narrower, predetermined scope.

Refine Ideas Between Rounds of the Tournament

Before moving the surviving opportunities to the next round of the innovation tournament, you should try to refine them. Although this can best be done by the person who initiated the idea, you might consider allowing participants to give rapid feedback. Quick comments of, say, fifty words each can have an enormous impact on the refinement of the idea. We've found that allowing time for people to jot down comments typically adds about three minutes to each vote. This is too time consuming in the initial round of a tournament but can be very helpful once you've narrowed your list to ten to thirty ideas.

Find Out What Works for You

In this chapter, we have outlined the architecture of a three-round screening process, starting with Web-based submissions and voting on hundreds of opportunities, then moving to an innovation workshop in which ideas are presented and again voted upon, ultimately leading to a detailed, multiattribute analysis of each opportunity. We have found this architecture to be very effective in a number of industries, ranging from professional services to the formation of start-ups. However, this tournament design is by no means written in stone, and it is possible to modify the design of the tournament to your specific business needs.

Some innovation settings foster dozens of opportunities, not hundreds. In such a situation, you might be better off bypassing Web-based voting and jumping immediately to an innovation workshop. Your workshop could start with a period dedicated to opportunity generation (either individually or in groups; see chapter 2) and then move directly to voting.

You can also combine elements of an innovation workshop and the Darwinator. You might ask workshop participants to generate opportunities while working in groups and then use the Darwinator for screening. You can also mix and match the tools for creating and filtering ideas. If your criteria are straightforward and easy to apply, you might begin the objective screening earlier in your tournament. If the criteria are more amorphous, you could base even the last round of your tournament on sticker voting. As long as the tournament consists of a sequence of filters, starting with efficient filters and ending with accurate ones, many modifications are possible.

SUMMARY

Given the tension between efficiency and accuracy in filtering, innovation tournaments should use multiple rounds of screening. The first round should stress efficiency and often works best when employing a Web-based voting tool like the Darwinator. Innovation workshops allow further filtering but in a way that lends itself to the refinement of opportunities. Finally, criteria-based screening corresponds to a checklist of what constitutes an exceptional opportunity worthy of investment. Just as a pilot works through a checklist before takeoff, so criteria such as the RWW list used by 3M ensure that you've considered everything critical before moving on. Criteria-based screening also makes explicit your strategic considerations. As we discuss in the next chapter, such strategic direction can substantially increase the quality of the average opportunity that you move forward. The result of smart screening should be a set of promising, practical opportunities—the best in each category—that you can move into development.

Diagnostics

- Do you have an opportunity screening process that filters many ideas, possibly hundreds? If not, is it because you don't have a large enough number of opportunities to begin with or because you do not use a deliberate process to pick the most promising opportunities?

- Have you organized innovation workshops to support the generation and screening of new opportunities? Have you worked with Web-based idea management systems?

- Who in your organization votes on opportunities or acts as an advocate for moving opportunities forward? What group dynamics exist in this process? Is there a way to anonymously express opinions or make suggestions?

- Do you have a set of criteria in your company to determine what kinds of innovations to seek and which ones to drop early in the process? Do they capture the essence of the RWW criteria? Are these criteria widely known in the organization?

- Do you divide opportunities into different categories reflecting their innovation horizon?

5

STRATEGIC FIT

Pulling Opportunities from Strategy

The previous chapters outlined a number of ways you can increase the supply of innovation opportunities and then screen them to find those that are exceptionally good. We implicitly assumed that any opportunity is a good thing and thus focused our attention on creating as many of them as possible. But, especially for established enterprises, innovation does not happen in a strategic vacuum. Competitors attempt to steal market share, technologies that once were cutting edge become obsolete, and markets that once were growing start to mature. This creates a demand for opportunities that address specific strategic needs—opportunities that strengthen one's competitive advantage, that explore the use of new technologies, or that create new markets and revitalize existing markets.

For this reason, innovation can be as much a *pull* process, directing the generation of new opportunities to where they will be of highest strategic value, as it is a *push* process, allowing a set of interesting opportunities to flow through a series of selection steps. Figure 5-1 illustrates the combination of these two approaches.

⇒ You can filter opportunities using strategic considerations as the criteria for screening and selection. By simply adding strategic considerations to the screening criteria discussed in the previous chapter, the opportunities that you generate might still range far and wide, yet the opportunities that you move forward will address important strategic needs.

⇒ Alternatively, you can attempt to direct the opportunity creation process to identify opportunities that are more likely to create strategic advantage in the first place. In this case, you communicate the strategic context and the gaps that you identified with the tools outlined in this chapter to those generating and sensing opportunities. We call this second approach *pulling opportunities from strategy*.

FIGURE 5-1

Strategy can be implemented by filtering opportunities according to strategic criteria, or strategy can pull the opportunity creation process by identifying specific innovation targets.

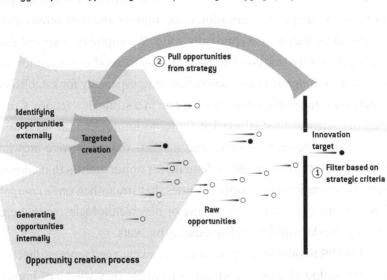

This chapter will provide you with a set of tools that help you with pulling opportunities from strategy. We explain how to conduct an innovation strategy audit that identifies areas in your company that are in need of innovation, thereby constituting important targets for future opportunity generation. We then discuss how the targets identified in the audit can be used to identify additional opportunities.

THE INNOVATION STRATEGY AUDIT

This chapter isn't a comprehensive review of business strategy—that's a subject for other authors and other books—but you should think in terms of overarching strategy as you answer the following questions:[1]

- *Who* are your company's target customers (market segments) and *why* do they buy from you?

- *What* products or services do you offer and *how* do they differ from the competition?

Keeping in mind that an innovation is a new match between a need and a solution, you can think of who and why as *needs*, and what and how as *solutions*. In answering these questions, you should be describing your firm's strategic intent. Unfortunately, this intent might not (and typically does not) correspond with the actual business situation. Markets and the economy change fast, and formerly market-leading products or services can quickly fall behind. This reality can create a set of strategic gaps that require innovations to close them.

An *innovation strategy audit* identifies existing and possible future gaps in your innovation portfolio. Gaps in the portfolio pull the appropriate opportunities forward instead of you pushing opportunities into the process. In the following two sections, we discuss how you can target your innovation gaps by assessing both the market's needs and your technological vitality. In gauging the market, you analyze your products or services *from your customers' point of view*, whereas in evaluating your technological position, you bore into the competitiveness of your technologies and determine where they stand in their life cycles.

THE MARKET NEED PERSPECTIVE

Start your innovation strategy audit by examining your product and service offerings through your customers' eyes. Think in terms of their needs. Ask yourself which attributes differentiate your products and services from your competitors. Ask which matter most to your customers and whether you're meeting or, better yet, exceeding their expectations. Finally, consider what your customers think when they buy (or, worse, don't buy) what you sell. The following three tools help you answer these questions.

The Value Map

Consider again the example of the iPod. In October 2001, when Apple launched the iPod, Diamond Multimedia's player, the Rio PMP300, had been on the market for more than three years. It, like most of its competitors, consisted of flash memory that was able to hold ten to thirty songs. The industry had commoditized quickly, bringing pressure to compete on price. None of the players stood out.

With the iPod, Apple launched a music player that ignored the conventional wisdom. It was larger, heavier, and, with a $400 price tag, triple the price of competitors. Yet it could hold one thousand songs and had a very fast PC connection and outstanding music management software (now known as iTunes). Apple's move fits an innovation approach called a *blue ocean strategy*.[2] Instead of battling in the existing market and competing on price, Apple redefined what mattered.

Value maps are used to pull the opportunity creation process by identifying a set of product attributes and evaluating the performance of competitors with respect to those attributes (figure 5-2). They help to detect obvious weaknesses in your products relative to your competition. But, as we discussed in chapter 2, innovation doesn't just reposition you in terms of existing product attributes. It tries to discover new sets of attributes. The opportunity creation process can then set its sights on identifying solutions that perform extremely well with respect to these underserved attributes, perhaps even at the expense of the traditional attributes. Simply replicating existing attributes satisfies your customers. Identifying new ones, as Apple did with the iPod, has the potential to delight them.

Analyze Attribute Positions Relative to Their Importance

Analyzing product attributes also can identify gaps between the hopes and expectations of customers and your ability to satisfy them with your current products and services. Unmet customer needs, especially those that haven't been explicitly articulated, are ideal targets for the opportunity creation process. Broad-based surveys can help

FIGURE 5-2

The graph compares the iPod and competing MP3 players with respect to a set of attributes. The big difference between the iPod and the competing products for the three attributes on the right suggests that the iPod created another dimension of merit, making the introduction of the player a "blue ocean strategy" move.

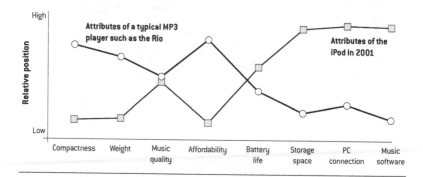

you zero in on these needs, especially when attempting to innovate in an established product category with a large existing customer base.

Another useful technique for identifying unmet needs is to plot the importance of a product or service attribute (or suite of them) with respect to the extent to which your product or service delivers on it. Figure 5-3 summarizes this approach for the curriculum of a major business school. The vertical axis shows student satisfaction with the school's current performance. The horizontal axis gives the students' assessment of the importance of the attributes. Looking at figure 5-3, we see that former students say the school delivers just about the right benefits relative to *drawing conclusions from data* but

FIGURE 5-3

Example performance-importance map for a business school. For each attribute the customer considers when purchasing the product or service, the firm compares its current position (as assessed by customers) and the importance of that attribute. Performance gaps are associated with attributes in the lower right of the graph.

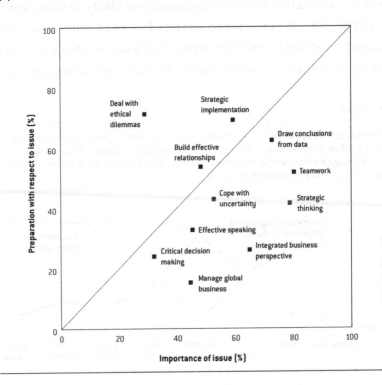

falls short on providing an *integrated business perspective*. Attributes that end up in the lower right corner of the figure—high in importance yet low in current performance—become targets in the opportunity creation process.

User Anthropology

You can also assess customer needs through observational studies of customers using your products. These studies (also called user anthropology or ethnography) provide a deeper understanding of true customer needs than you can obtain through surveys.

Consider the bicycle industry. Shimano, a maker of bike components such as pedals and brakes, recently commissioned a user anthropology study to understand why more people don't ride bikes. The traditional approach to this problem would have been to create a survey or a set of focus groups asking customers how often they ride and what attributes of a bike they value the most. Most likely, most Americans would say that they ride regularly (which for them might mean once a year) and that they want light bikes with many gears. Those, after all, are the product attributes emphasized in nearly every bike shop.

Unfortunately, what people say to researchers and what they really do can differ markedly. By spending many hours observing potential cyclists, including their time on and off bicycles, Shimano researchers found that many consumers want bikes that are technically simple, easy to ride, and easy to get on and off—all attributes that aren't emphasized in the current competition among bike makers, who tend to emphasize the needs of biking enthusiasts.

User anthropology thus helped Shimano to identify a set of *latent* needs.[3] Once a latent need is articulated, it becomes a target for the opportunity creation process. Note especially how such latent needs can help you redefine the value map discussed earlier. Once you have identified the latent needs that keep Americans in their SUVs as opposed to on their bikes, you have the opportunity to redefine the product category.

In the case of Shimano, these efforts led to the creation of bikes targeted specifically at the leisure rider, that is, people who might rent a bike during their annual family trip to the beach but otherwise don't ride regularly. Shimano developed a line of components under the brand Coasting, and manufacturers then incorporated them into their bikes. One example is the Trek Lime, shown in figure 5-4.

THE TECHNOLOGY SOLUTION PERSPECTIVE

In their efforts at addressing customer needs with new solutions, most firms tend to build deep expertise in some specific technologies (for example, combustion engines, Internet search algorithms, flavors and fragrances). This sort of expertise is required to identify new matches between needs and solutions, to translate these matches into product or service offerings, and to deliver the resulting offering to the customer.

FIGURE 5-4

The Trek Lime bicycle incorporates the Shimano Coasting component group.

Source: Trek Bicycle Corporation.

The following three tools let you analyze your current areas of expertise and help you identify targets for future opportunity generation.

Technology Positions

As a leading provider of energy and automation technologies, the Swiss-Swedish company ABB routinely evaluates its product lines. It assesses its market dominance, technology performance, costs, and intellectual property alongside those of its competitors. Figure 5-5 shows an easy way, used by ABB, of making these comparisons. The company refers to this method as the *traffic light approach*. The rows in the figure correspond to the firm's existing product lines. The *market position* column is black where ABB is the market leader, gray where it's one of the top five players, and white otherwise (to extend the traffic light analogy, make the colors green, yellow, and red). The *technology position* column evaluates your technology relative to competitors. Here, the criteria are specific to ABB, with its emphasis on technology leadership. A consumer-product manufacturer might use brand position instead of intellectual property position. The criteria should reflect your strategy by defining the areas in which you seek competitive advantage. The gray and white (yellow and red) lights then become targets for the opportunity creation process.

FIGURE 5-5

Traffic light analysis. For each product line or service offering of the firm, evaluate the current strategic position with respect to a set of criteria. The results can be visualized using different shades or colors.

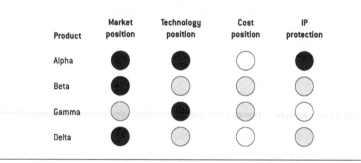

Core Competencies and Capabilities

Theories of competitive advantage abound, but most spring from the idea that firms achieve above-average profits by exploiting unique resources. *Resources,* an umbrella term, includes *capabilities*, *core competencies*, and *competitive advantage*. To provide advantage, a resource must be:[4]

⟹ **Valuable.** To be valuable, a resource must either allow a firm to achieve greater performance than a rival or reduce a weakness relative to a rival.

⟹ **Rare.** Given competition, a resource must be rare.

⟹ **Inimitable.** For value and rarity to persist, a resource must not be easily imitated.

⟹ **Nonsubstitutable.** Even if valuable, rare, and inimitable, a resource can't be easily substituted.

This perspective, abbreviated as VRIN, can be used to define targets by first articulating an inventory of resources and then using the inventory as a lens for opportunity creation.

Apple's VRIN resources, for example, might include excellence in industrial design, a leading brand, and a loyal customer base. Each of these resources can inspire a challenge in the opportunity creation process. In what other product categories might Apple's design excellence create advantage? For which product or service categories could the Apple brand be deployed to advantage? What other products or services could Apple provide to its customer base? Apple's recent introduction of the iPhone appears as a logical step given the capabilities defined earlier.

Technology Life Cycles

Technologies follow life cycles that display remarkably consistent patterns. Almost all new technologies start with slow sales growth, followed by an exponential surge, maturation, and then stabilization or decline.[5] Figure 5-6 shows the trajectory of music album sales over the last three decades. Initially, music was sold on large plastic discs that spun on turntables. But turntables were first displaced by cassette tape players and then by compact disc players. At the beginning of the twenty-first century, CD sales are falling (though still high in absolute numbers), and digital music distribution through outlets such as iTunes has begun to take off.

In most cases, an individual company can't resist the rise and fall of a technology. Sony, for example, may have wanted to continue to distribute music only on eight-track tapes, but to do so would have been a death sentence. At the beginning of the twenty-first century, no large entertainment company can afford to ignore online distribution. The targets of innovation change as a technology matures. Each stage of the technology life cycle offers new targets for the opportunity creation process:[6]

FIGURE 5-6

Most successful technologies experience the sales pattern illustrated in this graphic. Sales are initially low and then accelerate quickly. Ultimately, the technology is displaced and sales decline.

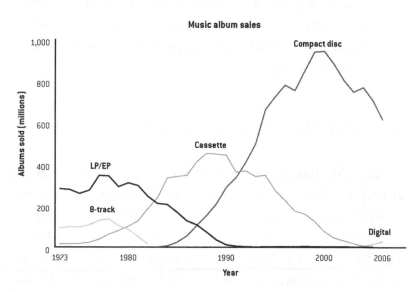

Source: Recording Industry Association of America.

➡ **Embryonic phase.** A characteristic of this period is the absence of a *dominant design*.[7] No technology has established itself as a standard. In this setting, the opportunity creation process should identify the rival technologies competing for dominance.

➡ **Growth.** Once a dominant design has taken hold, the amount of uncertainty falls. Along with the dominant design, *dimensions of merit*—key attributes that characterize product performance—emerge. The focus of opportunity creation is enhancing performance along the dimensions of merit.

➡ **Maturation.** The focus of competition shifts more and more to the efficiency of product delivery. Firms fight to gain scale and diversify their offerings to appeal to different market segments, yet they typically offer a similar basic technology. The automotive industry has been in this phase for almost a century. Here, opportunity creation should target cost efficiency and solutions that address subtle differences in customer needs.

➡ **Decline.** As a technology declines, some rival technology usually crops up. In this environment, you continue to focus on efficiency but should also seek new uses for the mature technology—so-called *last-gasp applications,* which can be surprisingly long lived.[8]

DIRECTING THE OPPORTUNITY CREATION PROCESS

So far, we've stressed how innovation strategy audits can help you identify gaps that then become targets for opportunity creation. But once you understand your gaps, you still have to feed that awareness back into your organization to ensure that you act on your new knowledge. We believe that the process of assessing gaps will lead to organizational awareness of needs and thus influence the process. Beyond this implicit influence, we see at least four means of direct influence.

⇒ **Establish opportunity generation projects with a focused charter.** Chapter 2 provides methods for generating opportunities internally. This activity requires only the dedication of time and will reliably produce many opportunities. Opportunity generation can be set up as a project with an ad hoc team assigned for a definite period. You can give the team a clear charter. One of us, for example, recently worked with a team charged with identifying horizon 2 opportunities for electrical products that could be sold through Home Depot and Lowe's. Even given such a narrow charter, the team identified about six hundred opportunities, three of which resulted in significant new products.

⇒ **Structure organization to address gaps.** Create an organizational unit with responsibility for your gaps. For example, a major producer of heating and cooling equipment faced difficulty in identifying far-horizon product opportunities. By creating an organizational unit with specific responsibility for creating, generating, and developing far-horizon opportunities, it filled that gap.

⇒ **Deploy sensing activities to address gaps.** Organizations create opportunities in part by sensing them externally. Gaps in the opportunity portfolio usually correspond to blind spots in the sensing network. A maker of children's products, for example, might address its gaps in part by tapping into user groups, blogs, and Web sites targeting parents and children. (See chapter 3 for more details.)

⇒ **Set quantitative goals by type of opportunity.** We asserted that simply assessing gaps is likely to influence the opportunity creation process. A slightly more aggressive intervention is to set quantitative goals for the fraction of opportunities identified of particular types. For example, a publishing company might set a goal that 25 percent of its opportunities should relate to electronic distribution. Such goals are somewhat arbitrary, but they serve as forces to influence the many organizational processes that generate and create opportunities.

SUMMARY

Two basic approaches enable you to identify opportunities aligned with your corporate strategy. You can filter a large set of opportunities using strategic considerations as the main criteria, or you can direct the opportunity creation process to identify opportunities that are likely to address strategic needs, in effect pulling opportunities from strategy.

You pull opportunities by identifying strategic targets for innovation. Your targets can then be used to influence the process of creating opportunities through organizational and administrative actions. This chapter discussed an array of analytical tools that help you in conducting innovation strategy audits.

The first three of these tools—the value map, the analysis of attribute positions, and user anthropology—consider innovation opportunities from the perspective of your customers. The other three—the traffic light, the analysis of competencies and capabilities, and the mapping of your technology life cycles—emphasize the role of solutions. Collectively, the tools contribute to an innovation strategy audit and help you to identify opportunities that are more likely to create strategic advantage.[9] They guide you in defining the scope of your innovation tournaments.

Diagnostics

How many of your innovation efforts follow a push approach and how many follow a pull approach?

➡ Do you understand your business strategy? Are you able to answer the questions related to the markets that you serve and the solutions that you offer?

➡ Do you routinely evaluate your market position and use this evaluation to identify gaps that then become the target for future innovation?

➡ Do you routinely evaluate your technology or solution position and use this evaluation to identify gaps that then become the target for future innovation?

➡ In what ways do you attempt to influence the opportunity creation process through the results of your innovation strategy audit?

SHORT-TERM PROFITABILITY

Analyzing Near-Horizon Opportunities

Innovation aims to create exceptional value. Deciding which of your opportunities is truly exceptional is thus a critical element of the innovation process. When opportunities are newly identified and only loosely articulated, you will select those with the most promise based on the subjective criteria outlined in chapter 4. But as you enter the later rounds of an innovation tournament, you should augment and enhance your subjective judgments with quantitative analysis.

This chapter describes tools for analyzing opportunities quantitatively in terms of financial value. Consider an example from the Swiss-Swedish power-and-automation company ABB. Figure 6-1 shows the expected returns for fourteen opportunities that the company considered, ranging from a new industrial robot to an innovation in power plants. The data are shown using the innovation return curve described in the introduction. A rectangle represents each project, with the width signifying the size of the required investment and the height its profitability. The profitability index in figure 6-1 is based on *expected profits,* that is, the forecast financial return from the project adjusted for the chances of success. *Actual profits* remain uncertain.

The first two projects (6 and 5) appear to be outstanding, with expected returns of more than ten times the required investment—truly exceptional opportunities. But then the return curve declines. The next opportunities are less profitable, though projects 12, 7, 10, and 11 still promise returns of more than five times the required investment. At the right end of the return curve, we see that projects 2 and 9 offer to pay back just a bit more than the required investment. These are thus the last projects of this set that ABB would fund. The

FIGURE 6-1

The innovation return curve is a way of representing opportunities in terms of their required investment and profitability. This example shows a set of ABB opportunities based on the expected values for investment and profits before the opportunities were pursued. Note that these projects were considered as a group because of their similarity, but reflect a small fraction of the opportunities pursued by the entire ABB organization.

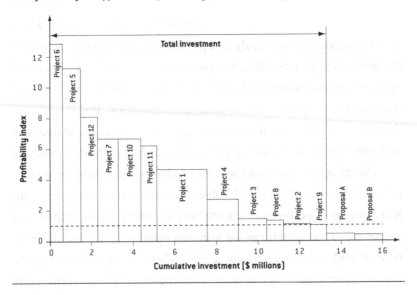

next two opportunities (proposals A and B) are below the bar because the expected returns do not exceed the required investment.

You can also construct a return curve *after* having pursued the opportunities and realized the payoffs. Figure 6-2 shows the actual return curve for the same set of opportunities. Note that both the required investments and the profitability deviate from the forecast. For example, project 10 beat project 5, even though the forecast predicted otherwise. Expected profits should exceed the required financial investments for all opportunities before you invest in them, but not all investments result in profits when you examine them afterward. For instance, projects are often canceled before launch, leading to a profitability index of zero. ABB killed project 9 before it was commercialized but not before it had consumed $1 million. Likewise, projects sometimes end up requiring more money than budgeted or sales fail to live up to forecasts.

FIGURE 6-2

This version of the return curve shows the ABB projects after the outcomes were realized and is based on actual returns and actual costs.

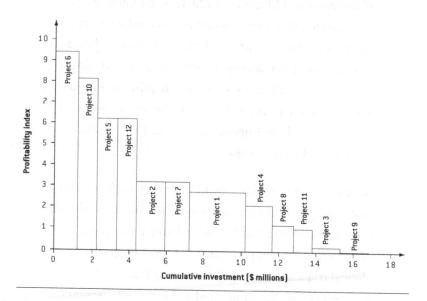

This chapter will help you estimate the expected returns from horizon 1 and horizon 2 opportunities so that you can construct a return curve like those shown earlier. Understand, however, that quantitative financial analysis is typically only useful for near-horizon opportunities (i.e., horizons 1 and 2), those for which there is only modest uncertainty about the prospects for an opportunity. For now, we'll focus on analyzing opportunities one at a time, assuming they are largely independent of each other. In chapter 7, we'll turn to the selection of a portfolio of opportunities, accounting for the interactions among opportunities from the perspective of the overall enterprise.

UNCERTAINTY ON THE NEAR AND FAR HORIZON

Chapter 4 defined the concept of horizon 1, horizon 2, and horizon 3 opportunities, a categorization based on level of uncertainty. The different horizons require different types of financial analysis.

⇒ **Horizon 1** opportunities carry limited risks. Consider Colgate's launch of a toothpaste called Colgate Tartar Protection Whitening Cool Mint Gel. Colgate won't know the exact sales, but it will have a good estimate based on its experience and purchase intent surveys. It will also have refined estimates of the costs of developing, producing, and marketing the toothpaste and the amount of time required before launch. The exact incremental sales level is the only major uncertainty. For horizon 1 opportunities like this, the main objective is to capture this *parameter uncertainty*.

⇒ **Horizon 2** opportunities present risks that are hefty enough that they could prompt the cancellation of the project either during development or following launch. For example, a pharmaceutical company such as Merck entering phase 2 clinical trials with a new diabetes drug faces a 65 percent probability that the compound will not reach the market.

The possibility of clinical failure haunts the endeavor. In analyzing horizon 2 opportunities, you emphasize capturing this *scenario uncertainty*.

➡ **Horizon 3** opportunities are so uncertain that you cannot even articulate a variety of outcome scenarios, let alone reduce the uncertainty to a single parameter. When the Virgin Group considers exploring the market for consumer space travel (Virgin Galactic), it does not even know what it does not know. Instead, it focuses on reducing uncertainty, where possible, to allow for better decision making. Here, Virgin faces "unknown unknowns."[1] (We treat this type of uncertainty in chapter 8.)

ANALYZING HORIZON 1 OPPORTUNITIES

When evaluating a horizon 1 opportunity, be it a new flavor of toothpaste, an upgrade to a software package, or the next season of a television show, you face uncertainty in the profits you will realize from further investment.

Consider the case of a project that requires an investment of $1.4 million and yields an expected profit of $3.2 million, giving an expected profitability index of 2.3 (i.e., $3.2 million/$1.4 million).[2] The return curve shows a single precise value for the profitability index, but in reality, this is just the *expected value* (the *average* outcome one would expect based on all the uncertainties associated with the project parameters).[3] Think instead of this uncertainty as a probability distribution over all of the possible outcomes, as shown in figure 6-3. The average outcome would be 2.3, but a whole range of outcomes was possible, and the actual one was 2.1.

Using some basic financial modeling tools, you can estimate a distribution of possible outcomes and use it to estimate the average outcome—the expected value. There are three steps to performing this analysis:

The profitability index of this project was expected to be 2.3, corresponding to a profit of $3.2 million on an investment of $1.4 million. However, uncertainty is always present, as reflected by the probability distribution shown in the figure. The actual realized value in this case was 2.1.

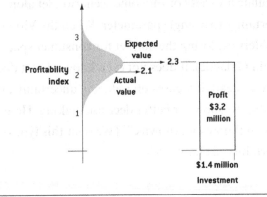

1. Build a financial model.

2. Model the uncertainty in the parameters.

3. Analyze the impact of the uncertainty on financial performance.

Build a Financial Model

You may already know how to create a financial model for a horizon 1 opportunity. You create a spreadsheet model and plug in assumptions about sales volume, price, cost of goods, required investments, discount rate, and the timing of these cash flows. Many textbooks explain how to do this.[4] Plus, your colleagues in the finance department of your company can probably help. This spreadsheet model does not explicitly capture the role of uncertainly but does capture the mathematical relationships between a given set of assumptions and an estimate of profitability.

Model the Uncertainty in the Parameters

Financial models require assumptions. You might assume, for example, that you will sell a certain quantity—but you can't know the outcome for sure. The extent of the uncertainty varies by parameter. (Figure 6-4 illustrates this uncertainty for the key parameters in the model for our project.) You're typically more certain, for example, about the cost of goods than about sales volume.

You can model uncertainty in at least three ways, and if possible, you should take all three approaches before making your assumptions. First, you can assign a probability distribution based on your experiences. Second, you can convene a group of experts and ask their opinions on the values of a parameter. You can then use the dispersion in their estimates as an indicator of the uncertainty you face. Third, you can look at the historical ratios of actual to forecast values for key parameters for similar opportunities from the past.

As an example of this third approach, consider the forecast and actual values for a set of twenty ABB projects, as shown in figure 6-5.

FIGURE 6-4

Uncertainty in parameters underlying the financial model for an innovation can be modeled and analyzed to estimate profitability and its associated uncertainty.

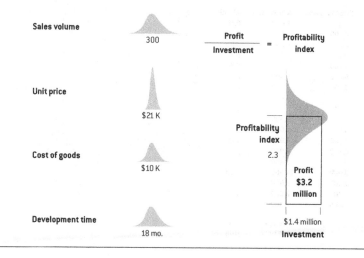

For each opportunity, we have computed the ratio between the *actual* sales and the *forecast* sales, providing an *actual–forecast (AF) ratio* for each opportunity. An AF ratio of 0.5 indicates that you overestimated demand: actual sales were half of what you forecast. A ratio of 1.5 indicates that the actual sales were 50 percent higher than forecast. Figure 6-5 includes a histogram of the AF ratios for the ABB projects. This histogram can be used as a model of the uncertainty you face in making a new forecast. You need a minimum of about fifteen opportunities and their forecasts for this sort of analysis.

Analyze the Impact of the Uncertainty on Financial Performance

You can analyze the impact of the uncertainty on your model parameters by using a method called Monte Carlo simulation. The simulation can be run directly from your spreadsheet model using software for that purpose such as Crystal Ball or @RISK. The soft-

FIGURE 6-5

The actual-forecast (AF) ratios for a set of ABB projects (left) and a histogram of those AF ratios (right).

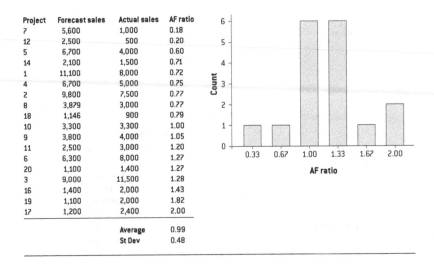

Project	Forecast sales	Actual sales	AF ratio
7	5,600	1,000	0.18
12	2,500	500	0.20
5	6,700	4,000	0.60
14	2,100	1,500	0.71
1	11,100	8,000	0.72
4	6,700	5,000	0.75
2	9,800	7,500	0.77
8	3,879	3,000	0.77
18	1,146	900	0.79
10	3,300	3,300	1.00
9	3,800	4,000	1.05
11	2,500	3,000	1.20
6	6,300	8,000	1.27
20	1,100	1,400	1.27
3	9,000	11,500	1.28
16	1,400	2,000	1.43
19	1,100	2,000	1.82
17	1,200	2,400	2.00
	Average	0.99	
	St Dev	0.48	

ware simply runs thousands of different scenarios, drawing values for the parameters randomly each time from the probability distributions you have assumed for the inputs. Then it creates a histogram of the outcome, which approximates the probability distribution of the output of the financial model. Figure 6-6 is the histogram for the model for the project discussed earlier in this chapter.

The figure shows that the project is likely to yield positive returns. Even so, it underscores that failure is possible: in about 2 percent of the cases the project loses money (profitability index below 1), and only in 20 percent does the profitability index exceed 3. The expected value of the project is still highly positive, however, and thus warrants investment. The result of this uncertainty modeling is

FIGURE 6-6

The histogram of profitability index based on one thousand runs of a simulation of the financial model of the project.

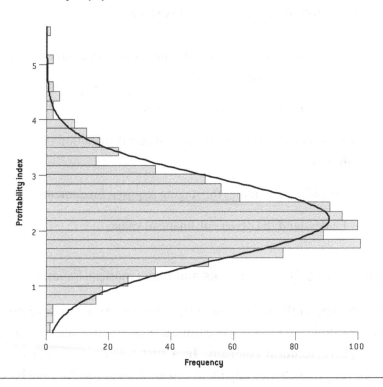

that you can be confident that this project will yield positive financial returns across many scenarios.

The results of your uncertainty analysis can also inform the tasks you plan for developing an opportunity. Indeed, a good development strategy (discussed in greater detail in chapter 8) is to complete first those tasks that reduce the uncertainty that clouds your understanding of the value of an opportunity.[5]

EVALUATING HORIZON 2 OPPORTUNITIES

When evaluating a horizon 2 opportunity, you face scenario uncertainty. Will the new compound be more effective than other treatments for hypertension? Will the government regulate fuel economy standards? Will the Internet become the primary means of video delivery?

We recommend a structured approach to financial analysis for horizon 2 opportunities comprising five steps:

1. Define a set of discrete events and the financial parameters associated with those events.

2. Estimate probabilities of the events.

3. Summarize the results in a probability distribution of returns.

4. Consider possibilities for staging required investments.

5. Understand the drivers of financial value.

Define a Set of Discrete Events and Their Financial Payoffs

The first step outlines the most likely scenarios. As an example, consider the following case of a chemical compound being evaluated by a pharmaceutical company. In a first round of clinical trials (phase 1), researchers study the compound's toxicity. At this phase, the chemical might show low toxicity, medium toxicity, or be so toxic that people can't tolerate it.

If humans can tolerate the treatment, it moves to the second round of clinical trials (phase 2). Here, researchers determine how effective the compound is with respect to curing specific diseases. For this specific compound, there are two possible outcomes: the efficacy is either medium or high.

This creates a total of five possible scenarios, each with an associated payoff.

⇒ Too toxic to tolerate, with no payoff. All trials are thus terminated.

⇒ Medium toxicity and high efficacy, with a payoff of $100 million.

⇒ Both medium toxicity and efficacy, with no payoff. The medium efficacy doesn't warrant the strong side effects that come with medium toxicity.

⇒ Low toxicity and medium efficacy, with a payoff of $100 million.

⇒ Low toxicity and high efficacy, with a payoff of $500 million. This is the jackpot, a compound with limited side effects because of its low toxicity, yet exhibiting high efficacy.

We can summarize these five scenarios as shown in figure 6-7. The graphs depicted in the figure are called *event trees* and summarize the possible outcomes as well as the payoffs. The two event trees are equivalent. Both end with five leaves, corresponding to the five potential outcomes and payoffs. The tree on the right, however, also provides information on the intermediate outcomes of the phase 1 clinical trials. For reasons that will become apparent soon, event trees with such intermediate outcomes better support some of the calculations discussed in this chapter, so we generally recommend that you use this format over the "flat" tree format displayed on the left.

116   INNOVATION TOURNAMENTS

FIGURE 6-7

Two event trees summarizing the possible scenarios and the associated payoffs for a new compound. The event tree on the right makes explicit the fact that the project is composed of two phases and shows the outcomes of the phases separately.

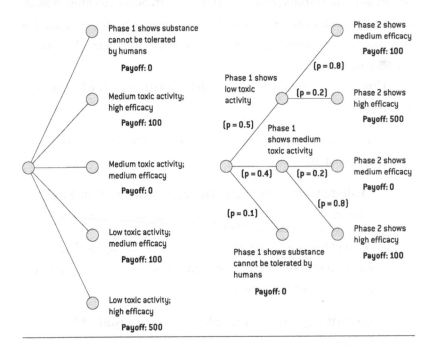

Estimate Probabilities of Success

After outlining the possible scenarios, you next estimate the probabilities of each. Our estimates of the probabilities of each scenario are shown in parentheses in figure 6-7. Because horizon 2 opportunities often have scenarios related to success and failure, the probability of the desired outcome is often referred to as *probability of success,* or POS for short. Estimating a probability is a tricky endeavor—as we'll discuss later in this chapter—and can have dramatic implications for the financial valuation of the opportunity.

Generally, you can choose among three POS estimation methods, which are similar to the methods for estimating parameter uncertainty for horizon 1 opportunities. First, you can use *historical data.* Table 6-1, for example, shows a set of probabilities for a variety

TABLE 6-1

Historical probability of success (POS) at each clinical milestone for a historical sample of compounds submitted to a regulatory body for approval.

Indication/disease	Phase 1	Phase 2	Phase 3
Alzheimer's disease	0.08	0.24	0.37
Anxiety disorders	0.01	0.07	0.17
Arrhythmias	0.02	0.06	0.29
Asthma	0.20	0.30	0.78
Attention-deficit hyperactivity disorder	0.39	0.54	0.72
Breast cancer	0.41	0.48	0.89
Cardiovascular disorders	0.27	0.45	0.75
Chronic obstructive pulmonary disease	0.25	0.42	0.73
Congestive heart failure	0.27	0.47	0.64
Depression	0.09	0.26	0.48
Diabetes mellitus	0.18	0.35	0.60
Epilepsy	0.17	0.39	0.65
Erectile dysfunction	0.48	0.60	0.80
Gastric ulcer	0.27	0.38	0.75
HIV-1 infections	0.17	0.32	0.63
Hepatitis B	0.71	0.77	0.97
Leukemia	0.38	0.51	0.89
Migraine	0.27	0.45	0.72
Multiple sclerosis	0.13	0.30	0.50
Ovarian cancer	0.19	0.30	0.65
Pain	0.36	0.48	0.85
Parkinson's disease	0.28	0.46	0.70
Postmenopausal osteoporosis	0.49	0.69	0.84
Schizophrenia	0.29	0.38	0.85
Stroke	0.07	0.23	0.34
Thrombosis	0.14	0.31	0.65
Ulcerative colitis	0.10	0.24	0.43

Sources: K. Girotra, C. Terwiesch, and K. Ulrich, "Risk Management in New Product Portfolios: A Study of Late Stage Drug Failures," *Management Science* 53, no. 3 (2007): 1452–1466 and ADIS International.

of drugs at each stage in the development process.[6] Given that the POS data show significant differences across illnesses, you would want to group the data points of prior opportunities according to illness. The main strength of forecasting POS using historical data is that your judgment is informed by evidence and you can resist an overconfidence bias in your decision making. However, this approach also assumes that the future will resemble the past.

A second method for obtaining a probability of success is an *aggregation of expert opinions*. Just as you have seen with the voting at the screening stage and the expert forecasts for horizon 1 opportunities, this approach begins with the experts creating independent forecasts. They then discuss their results, typically forming a consensus forecast. Alternatively, you can simply average their estimates, or you can designate an experienced expert to play the role of oracle— Merck uses this approach.[7] The oracle listens to all arguments and translates them into a single number. Unlike historical data, expert opinions can look forward, factoring in the idiosyncrasies of the opportunity. However, they also can become mired in the usual human biases and blind spots.

A third way to get your POS is to use *explicit criteria* of what is required for an opportunity to be labeled a 50 percent success probability. Procter & Gamble, for example, has found that by using explicit criteria that lay out what corresponds to, say, a 50 percent POS, expert discussion can focus more on facts and less on opinions.[8] For example, criteria might include the purchase intent results derived from a concept test, the extent to which the innovation deviates from existing products, and the extent to which the market is currently served by the company. The explicit criteria give some structure to the conversation about uncertainty, but defining the criteria consumes a lot of time. Even more time gets spent translating the criteria to numeric probabilities.

There is no one right way to forecast POS. Use multiple approaches and understand that you face an extra level of risk if these approaches deliver very different estimates. You should also test your analysis for its sensitivity to changes in the POS forecast: if a small reduction in POS turns your healthy return into a loss, the opportunity is probably not worth funding.

Create a Distribution of Potential Payoffs

Combining the payoffs with the probabilities allows you to compute the expected payoff of an opportunity. In our case of the new medication, the expected payoff (not yet including the necessary investment) can be calculated as follows.

$$
\begin{aligned}
\text{Expected payoff} = {} & \text{Prob(no payoffs)} \times 0 \\
& + \text{Prob(\$100 million)} \times 100 \\
& + \text{Prob(\$500 million)} \times 500 \\[6pt]
= {} & (0.1 + 0.4 \times 0.2) \times 0 \\
& + (0.5 \times 0.8 + 0.4 \times 0.8) \times 100 \\
& + (0.5 \times 0.2) \times 500 \\[6pt]
= {} & \$122 \text{ million}
\end{aligned}
$$

Thus, the expected payoff from this opportunity is $122 million. Now you factor in the required investment in the opportunity. In this case, the development costs $30 million for the phase 1 trials and $100 million for the phase 2 trials. You end up with a net gain (loss) of $122 million – $130 million = –$8 million.

As with horizon 1 opportunities, you can also analyze the distribution of payoffs for the project, as shown in figure 6-8. Although the expected payoff is negative, there exists a 10 percent probability of a significant gain. Should you invest in this opportunity, despite its negative payoffs?

Consider Possibilities for Staging the Required Investment

So far, we've treated the $130 million as a one-shot investment: you either spend the money or you don't. This ignores the fact that you can

FIGURE 6-8

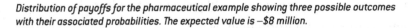

Distribution of payoffs for the pharmaceutical example showing three possible outcomes with their associated probabilities. The expected value is −$8 million.

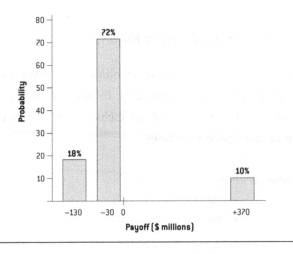

make an intermediate decision after obtaining information from phase 1 but before making the additional, larger investment in phase 2. Factoring in your ability to kill the project (that is, to not spend the money on phase 2) in case of a negative phase 1 outcome greatly increases the value of the opportunity.

To see this logic, consider the three possible outcomes of the phase 1 trials:

➡ **Case 1 (low toxicity).** When you learn about the outcome of phase 1, you have already spent $30 million. These costs are what economists call *sunk*—the money is gone, and you can't recoup it, so it's no longer relevant to your analysis. If you learn that the toxicity is low, you can expect to earn a payoff after phase 2 of 0.8 × $100 million + 0.2 × $500 million = $180 million. For this, you would have to spend another $100 million. Would you do this? The answer is an enthusiastic yes. This investment would be expected to create $80 million in value.

⇒ **Case 2 (medium toxicity).** When you learn about medium toxicity in phase 1, you again should look forward, not backward. What matters is that you have an expected payoff of $80 million (0.2 × $0 + 0.8 × $100 million), not that you have spent $30 million. This is especially important when deciding on the next $100 million investment. Investing $100 million to obtain an expected $80 million destroys value. So, as painful as it might be having spent $30 million for nothing, you kill the project.

⇒ **Case 3 (too toxic to tolerate).** Again, the $30 million is sunk and, because you have no hope of making any money going forward, you should terminate the project after phase 1.

Now let's return to the decision to initiate phase 1 trials. The calculations are summarized in figure 6-9. Is this project a good investment? You have a 50 percent shot at $80 million and a 50 percent (i.e., 40% + 10%) shot at nothing, so the expected profit is $40 million. For this, you have to spend $30 million for the phase 1 trials. Now what originally looked like a bad investment looks much better—a $40 million payoff for a $30 million investment. Note also that this investment is now less risky, because you have eliminated the scenario in which you suffer a $130 million loss. This analysis reveals why we advocated the event tree with the intermediate outcomes in our discussion of figure 6-7.

The example leads to two overarching observations about innovation investments. First, most of them happen in phases, and the early phases are usually less expensive than the later ones. Although the first phases by themselves typically do not lead to financial rewards, they provide something almost as valuable: information. Second, when investing in a new opportunity, remember that you can walk away if the information you gather points to failure. Failing is part of innovation, and failing early makes more sense than failing late. Ditching an opportunity is often referred to as an *exit option*.[9] As experienced innovators say, "Fail often, fail early, and fail inexpensively."

FIGURE 6-9

The decision tree for phase 1, making explicit the option to terminate the project and therefore not make the phase 2 investment of $80 million.

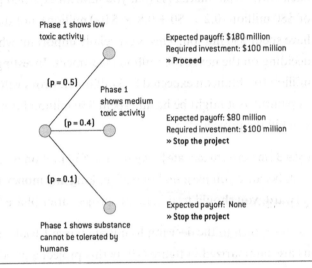

Phase 1 shows low toxic activity

Expected payoff: $180 million
Required investment: $100 million
» **Proceed**

(p = 0.5)

Phase 1 shows medium toxic activity

(p = 0.4)

Expected payoff: $80 million
Required investment: $100 million
» **Stop the project**

(p = 0.1)

Expected payoff: None
» **Stop the project**

Phase 1 shows substance cannot be tolerated by humans

Understanding the Drivers of Financial Value

Once you have outlined all of the ingredients for the calculations in figure 6-7, valuing the compound is a matter of arithmetic. The calculation itself turns out to be simple. The harder problem is getting the numbers required for the inputs.

To see the importance of your assumptions in the payoff calculations, consider again the examples described in figure 6-7. By redoing the calculations with slightly lower (or higher) estimates for the probability of obtaining a medium toxicity, we learn the sensitivity of the results to the assumptions. In this case, a 1 percentage point increase in probability (for example, a move in the probability from 50 percent to 51 percent) is worth $0.8 million in value, which corresponds to roughly 10 percent of the overall value of the innovation. Changing the probability from 50 percent to 60 percent increases project value by 100 percent.

The specific magnitude of POS estimates can have a dramatic effect on your decisions. For this reason, we recommend that you do the computations outlined earlier with a range of plausible success probabilities, not just one. If the opportunity is profitable only for a small range of probabilities, you probably should skip it.

Representing Horizon 2 Opportunities on the Return Curve

When several different scenarios could play out, each with a different investment profile, characterizing an opportunity on the return curve is a little tricky. Should the required investment you show (i.e., the width of the rectangle representing the opportunity) be the *first* infusion of capital or the expected spending over the life of the opportunity, factoring in the chances of the subsequent rounds of investment? The answer depends on how you use your return curve. If you use it to think about what your innovation budget ought to be for the next year, then you might restrict the required investment to be what you expect to need over the next year. Otherwise, you probably ought to set the value for the required investment to be the total you expect to invest over the life of the project, factoring in the probabilities of each of the scenarios.

SUMMARY

The objective of opportunity analysis is to assign financial values to opportunities and to identify the types and sources of risk. When possible, you should aim to include the computation of an expected return as well as an analysis of its variance to capture the financial risk associated with the investment.

Horizon 1 opportunities entail parameter uncertainty. You're confident that they will make it to market and generate revenue—you just don't know how much. The biggest obstacle in evaluation is an overly optimistic sales forecast. By analyzing your prior forecasts, you can see whether they're consistently overly optimistic. You then can also quantify their variance by comparing the forecasts to your actual results. Alternatively, you can empanel expert forecasters to do an analysis for you.

Horizon 2 opportunities risk failure: your ideal scenario may not play out. When valuing a horizon 2 opportunity, you should stage your investment: spend a little—learn a lot. This way, you quickly gather information and can make the bigger, later decisions with far less uncertainty.

Financial evaluation of innovation opportunities requires that you wrestle with fuzzy numbers—subjective evaluations, forecasts, and relatively unsupported assumptions. To increase your confidence in the analysis, you should attempt to estimate payoffs or success probabilities using several methods. Exceptionally good opportunities are so clearly above the line that their analysis indicates strong financial returns even under very conservative assumptions and across an array of different financial models.

Diagnostics

- What measures do you use to evaluate the financial attractiveness of opportunities? Do you distinguish between different horizons?

- Do you use measures for the probability of success? How are these probabilities computed?

- Does your company keep data on old forecasts with respect to financial returns, sales volume, and probability of success?

- When analyzing the financials of a new opportunity, do you factor in how previous forecasts fared?

- Are you able to spot weak opportunities early on, or do your opportunities tend to linger, regardless of their prospects, once they have started development?

- Do you use analytical tools such as event trees and Monte Carlo simulation?

7

INTERDEPENDENCE

Forming Opportunity Portfolios

Imagine that you're a coach charged with assembling an Olympic soccer team. Would you simply recruit the eleven best players available? What if five were goalies? What if all eleven had outstanding talent but little match experience? You can't maximize the success of a soccer team by hiring the best individual players. In the same way, you don't obtain the best innovation portfolio by picking those opportunities that are—in isolation—the most valuable. Considering each opportunity independently and simply selecting the most valuable ones fails because of *interdependencies* among them. Portfolio management, therefore, is about understanding interdependencies.

Consider the pharmaceutical company Merck. It periodically selects a portfolio of compounds for preclinical development. Table 7-1 lists a set of thirty candidates along with an estimate of each one's probability of success and its financial payoff, if successful.[1] For example, compound A, a drug targeted toward the respiratory market,

TABLE 7-1

A set of compounds considered for further preclinical development at Merck. The payoff listed is the expected profit contribution if the compound eventually is proven safe and effective and is approved for sale. POS is the probability of success through phase 3 clinical trials.

Compound	Indication	POS	Payoff ($ millions)
A	Respiratory 1	0.18	847
B	Respiratory 1	0.10	847
C	Respiratory 2	0.15	726
D	Obesity 1	0.20	2,643
E	Obesity 1	0.18	2,643
F	Obesity 2	0.15	4,650
G	Obesity 2	0.10	4,650
H	Depression 1	0.15	1,875
I	Depression 1	0.13	1,875
J	Metabolic disorder 1	0.16	1,347
K	Metabolic disorder 1	0.16	1,347
L	Cardiac 1	0.22	423
M	Cardiac 1	0.14	423
N	Cardiac 2	0.13	608
O	Alzheimer's 1	0.13	769
P	Alzheimer's 1	0.17	769
Q	Parkinson's 1	0.10	1,452
R	Osteoporosis 1	0.19	460
S	Osteoporosis 1	0.17	460
T	Pain 1	0.18	862
U	Pain 1	0.15	862
V	Pain 2	0.15	2,014
W	AIDS 1	0.10	417
X	AIDS 1	0.07	417
Y	Diabetes 1	0.20	2,226
Z	Diabetes 1	0.18	2,226
AA	Diabetes 1	0.16	2,226
BB	Diabetes 1	0.17	2,226
CC	Diabetes 2	0.18	3,865
DD	Diabetes 2	0.11	3,865

has a POS of 18 percent and would contribute profits of $847 million if eventually successful.

Assuming that Merck can select twenty of the thirty compounds, given its capacity constraints for the coming year, it could just compute the *expected* payoff for each one by multiplying the POS times the payoff and then simply pick those with the highest risk-adjusted payoffs. This approach is illustrated in figure 7-1, showing the expected payoffs for each of the thirty opportunities in a return-curve format, assuming that the required investment for each compound is the same. Diabetes and obesity drugs offer the greatest return, and logic would dictate that Merck select those for further development.

Although it is a useful tool for visualizing the opportunities, the return curve does not capture interdependencies among them—it looks at the returns (the profitability index) of each one in isolation. If we pick opportunities based on profitability index alone, we might end up with three obesity drugs and nothing for depression. That would be like forming a soccer team with five goalies and no offense.

At least five types of interdependencies are of importance to the management of an innovation portfolio:

- **Market cannibalization.** If you target four opportunities that satisfy the same consumer need, you won't typically quadruple your sales. Despite Pixar's success with the movie *Finding Nemo*, it's unlikely that it could launch another one called *Finding Sam: The Story of a Small Camel Lost in the Desert* in the same season. The opposite effect may also play out: multiple opportunities in the same industry or product category may allow the firm to own the market and achieve greater success than might arise from the sum of the parts.

- **Balancing exploitation and exploration.** Some opportunities, especially those that we labeled horizon 3 opportunities in previous chapters, are exploratory. They may not directly create value but instead open up future possibilities. A firm with only horizon 1 opportunities might be ill-prepared for

FIGURE 7-1

Return curve for the thirty compounds in table 7-1, assuming the same required investment for each compound.

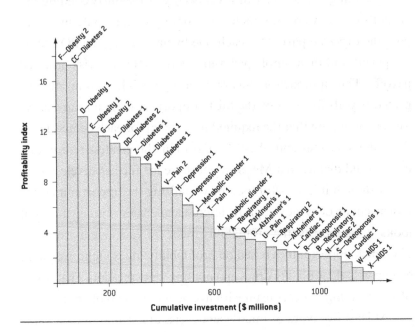

the future, but one with only horizon 3 opportunities may not live long enough to see it.[2]

⇒ **Smoothing revenues.** Most companies prefer to grow at a smooth and constant rate instead of facing big swings in revenues, even if the long-term trend is the same.

⇒ **Smoothing demands on resources.** Several opportunities might require access to the same scarce resource. If you fund multiple opportunities that demand this resource, you might have to delay some of them or reduce their share of the resource. A pharmaceutical company, for example, may have limited capacity for analyzing data from clinical trials and, as a result, may choose to pursue opportunities for which it can handle the analysis in a timely fashion.

➥ **Hedging against external risks.** Some opportunities are valuable in combination with others because, taken together, they are a hedge against external risks. You might select your portfolio of opportunities based on the extent to which they cover major risks. This is analogous to a diversification strategy in a financial portfolio.

This chapter outlines methods for constructing a valuable opportunity portfolio. To that end, we introduce five portfolio planning tools, one for each of the five interdependencies just discussed.

MARKET CANNIBALIZATION

Four obesity drugs will not produce four times more revenue for Merck than one obesity drug. To the extent that multiple opportunities address the same or similar market needs, they cannot be evaluated independently.

At first glance, addressing this interdependency is easy. You just pick the opportunity with the greatest potential in each market segment. Unfortunately, this strategy could leave you with no viable product in a lucrative market, in the event that your initial opportunity fails. For this reason, you should sometimes develop similar opportunities in parallel. Drug companies address this challenge by designating one compound a *lead* and the others *backups*. When considering multiple opportunities in the same market, you can sometimes control the type of risk you are taking. You might minimize technology risk by betting on two opportunities addressing the same need with different technological approaches. Or you might mitigate market risk by betting on two opportunities that present different bundles of features and benefits to the same group of consumers.

To avoid market cannibalization while ensuring that you cover every market segment, employ a *market segmentation map*. Figure 7-2 shows such a map for four medical needs represented in table 7-1. The chart shows the size of the market segments and how well the

FIGURE 7-2

A market segmentation map for four medical indications included in table 7-1. The areas of
the circles are proportional to the estimated payoffs for the markets. The shaded compound
is the lead compound, and the others are backups. Compounds represented within a
segment by the same shape belong to the same molecular family and thus share some
risk factors related to similar underlying biological mechanisms.

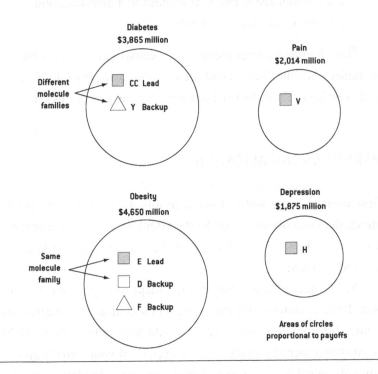

segments are covered by the portfolio of opportunities. Note that in
the case of the most attractive segments—diabetes and obesity—
backups are included in the portfolio to increase the odds of having a
drug reach the market. Merck could use Monte Carlo simulation, as
discussed in chapter 6, to further optimize the portfolio, including
the appropriate number of backups for each segment.

BALANCING EXPLOITATION AND EXPLORATION

In whaling's nineteenth-century heyday, whale oil lamps lit millions of
American homes. But whale oil production achieved a peak around

1850 when competing technologies—"town gas" and kerosene— emerged. In less than ten years, households almost fully abandoned whale oil for illumination, as figure 7-3 shows.[3] The dominance of kerosene lamps didn't last long either. In 1879, Edison's electric lamp began to make its way. What could a whale-oil producer have done to cope with these new competitors? Could it have explored far-horizon opportunities such as kerosene and electricity? Maybe no whale-oil company could have weathered changes as radical as these. But all products and industries experience life cycles. The key question in selecting an innovation portfolio is how to balance the exploration of new opportunities with the exploitation of existing ones.

Consider again the iPod, which Apple introduced in October 2001. It was a late entry into what at that time was a competitive MP3 player market. Diamond Multimedia had been selling its player, the Rio PMP300, for more than three years. At the time, almost all players consisted of flash memory that held ten to thirty songs. The industry

FIGURE 7-3

The rise and fall of whale-based oil production in the United States.

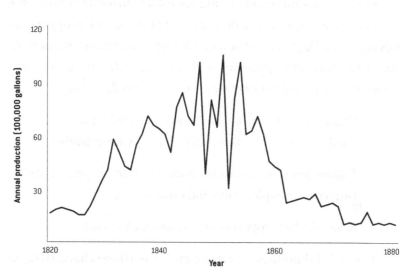

Source: Amory B. Lovins et al., *Winning the Oil Endgame* (Snowmass, CO: Rocky Mountain Institute, 2004). Original data were compiled by U.S. Commission of Fish and Fisheries, *The Fisheries and Fishery Industries of the United States* (Washington, D.C.: Government Printing Office, 1887).

had commoditized quickly, and companies competed on price. Other differentiators were battery life and size, but none of the players had been able to distinguish itself.

With the iPod, Apple offered a product that defied conventional wisdom. It was larger and heavier than other players, and at $400, triple the price. Yet it also had a thousand-song capacity, a very fast PC connection, and outstanding music management software (now known as iTunes). As discussed in chapter 4, Apple's move fits an innovation strategy referred to as a *blue ocean strategy:* instead of battling in the existing market based on price and established dimensions of merit, Apple redefined what mattered in a music player.[4]

At the time, the music-related innovation didn't seem to fit Apple's strategy of creating high-end computers for professionals and educators. But with relatively little investment, the company managed to explore a new territory and create for itself the option of shifting strategy. The iPod was a wedge into the world of handheld computers. At the time of this writing, Apple has begun to exercise this option through the development and expansion of its iPhone and related devices, which have the potential to be a growth engine for a decade or longer.

Options for future exploitation are most valuable in the presence of great uncertainty, so you should invest in at least a few opportunities in areas of high market and technology uncertainty, that is, horizon 3 territory. One planning tool that will help you create such options is the *strategic bucket method*, which has three steps:

1. Define several strategic buckets corresponding to combinations of market and technology uncertainty.

2. Budget resources across the buckets, reflecting your relative emphasis on exploitation and exploration.

3. Select the best opportunities within each bucket.

Figure 7-4 illustrates a strategic bucket portfolio chart. Here, an established car company groups nine combinations of market and technology novelty into three buckets, corresponding to our earlier defi-

FIGURE 7-4

A firm should consider opportunities in familiar areas (lower left) but also explore new territory, thereby creating options for future strategic moves. Project examples for a large automotive firm are shown in italics.

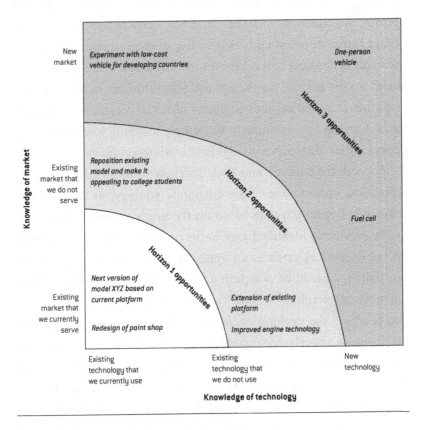

nition of the three horizons. Incremental innovations (horizon 1), such as improvements in painting or tweaks to existing models, receive 60 percent of the company's innovation resources. Growth opportunities in adjacent markets and improved technologies (horizon 2) get 30 percent. Exploratory opportunities (horizon 3), such as a one-person transporter, an experimental fuel cell, or an emerging market, receive the rest. Although in this example the strategic buckets happen to correspond to the three horizons, other categorization schemes for the buckets are possible.

The strategic bucket framework helps firms to achieve a balance between protection of their current position and the creation of future options. It has three strengths. First, by simply mapping out all current innovation activities in the firm, it helps you quickly spot the obvious, yet common, mistakes of either focusing too much on the distant future or investing mostly in line extensions without making the small but critical bets on the future.[5] We know of no methods or guidelines for quantifying the optimal allocation across buckets for a given firm (e.g., should your company spend 10 percent or 15 percent on far-horizon opportunities?). But simply mapping your innovation opportunities often serves to highlight obvious problems.

Second, the bucket framework dovetails with the idea of pulling innovation opportunities from corporate strategy, as described in chapter 5. Bucket sizes are based on the firm's growth strategy and on the previously identified gaps in the portfolio. Third, the strategic bucket framework ensures an apples-to-apples comparison of opportunities. Instead of comparing the opportunity "explore emerging markets for vehicle x" with "improve the paint shop utilization," you compare the exploration of fuel-cell technology with, say, the possibility of a purely electric vehicle. Be aware, however, that this third advantage is also a weakness of the bucket framework. It requires that the resource allocation for each strategic bucket be made *independently* of the opportunities available for funding in other buckets. Thus, you might end up funding a marginal opportunity in bucket 1 while abandoning an attractive one in bucket 2.

SMOOTHING REVENUES

Most companies would prefer to launch one opportunity per year instead of two every other year. The reason for this is that firms have substantial fixed costs in the form of employees, labs, studios, or equipment. Utilization of these resources usually depends on revenues, and resources are sticky: they cannot easily be adjusted upward

ations launched each
infer required flow rates

2013	2014
110	108
40	45
25	40
15	25
10	15
5	10
205	5
	248

1
2 → 1
2
3   2

New 6

olio planning
ordinating the
that lead to these

get growth rate and
to innovation tourna-
sized firm currently has
se revenues to $248 mil-
ce one major new product
each product line will grow
ar to $40 million in the fifth
aments with four phases (with
phase 4 being the last stage).
launches, it can work backward
opportunities that will be required
n process. These are calculated from
of the innovation tournaments. These
om the success probabilities. We discuss
abilities in chapter 6. If the filter ratio at
ortunities must exit phase 3 to support one
se 4. By similar logic, and based on the filter
-5, the firm will need to operate its innovation
y-six opportunities exit phase 1 each year. Let's
ore the obvious. Revenue forecasts like these are
But the analysis forces the firm to reconcile as-
growth with the creation and development of oppor-
port that growth.
e perspective of portfolio planning, the revenue pipeline
w resources should be allocated across the innovation
maximize the chances that revenues will grow smoothly. It
ou to reconcile revenue growth goals with the investments re-
upstream. You cannot expect double-digit growth without
ag previously planted the seeds of innovation opportunities in
or years.

FIGURE 7-5

The revenue pipeline is constructed from assumptions about innov
year. The filter ratios for the innovation phases can then be used to
at each phase of the innovation process.

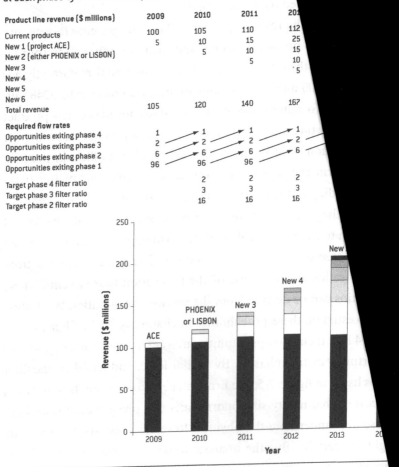

Product line revenue ($ millions)	2009	2010	2011	20?
Current products	100	105	110	112
New 1 (project ACE)	5	10	15	25
New 2 (either PHOENIX or LISBON)		5	10	15
New 3			5	10
New 4				˙5
New 5				
New 6				
Total revenue	105	120	140	167
Required flow rates				
Opportunities exiting phase 4	1	1	1	1
Opportunities exiting phase 3	2	2	2	2
Opportunities exiting phase 2	6	6	6	6
Opportunities exiting phase 1	96	96	96	
Target phase 4 filter ratio		2	2	2
Target phase 3 filter ratio		3	3	3
Target phase 2 filter ratio		16	16	16

SMOOTHING RESOURCE USE

The revenue pipeline is a top-down approach to planning. You can also take a bottom-up approach and examine the capacity of your resources and the demands imposed on them by opportunities under consideration. Pixar Animation Studios, creator of such hits as *Toy* or downward without significant expense. The portfolio planning tool that helps you achieve a target growth rate by coordinating the launches of innovations as well as the tournaments that lead to these innovations is called the *revenue pipeline*.

To see how the revenue pipeline takes a target growth rate and translates it into product launches and then into innovation tournaments, consider the following case. A medium-sized firm currently has revenues of $100 million and plans to increase revenues to $248 million by 2014. To achieve this, it will introduce one major new product line a year starting in 2009. It expects that each product line will grow from $5 million of sales in the first year to $40 million in the fifth year. The firm runs innovation tournaments with four phases (with phase 1 leading to the first filter and phase 4 being the last stage).

Once the firm has planned the launches, it can work backward from them to calculate the flow of opportunities that will be required in each phase of the innovation process. These are calculated from the filter ratios at each phase of the innovation tournaments. These filter ratios can be derived from the success probabilities. We discuss how to estimate these probabilities in chapter 6. If the filter ratio at phase 4 is 2, then two opportunities must exit phase 3 to support one opportunity exiting phase 4. By similar logic, and based on the filter ratios listed in figure 7-5, the firm will need to operate its innovation process so that ninety-six opportunities exit phase 1 each year. Let's pause and underscore the obvious. Revenue forecasts like these are highly uncertain. But the analysis forces the firm to reconcile assumed revenue growth with the creation and development of opportunities to support that growth.

From the perspective of portfolio planning, the revenue pipeline dictates how resources should be allocated across the innovation phases to maximize the chances that revenues will grow smoothly. It forces you to reconcile revenue growth goals with the investments required upstream. You cannot expect double-digit growth without having previously planted the seeds of innovation opportunities in prior years.

FIGURE 7-5

The revenue pipeline is constructed from assumptions about innovations launched each year. The filter ratios for the innovation phases can then be used to infer required flow rates at each phase of the innovation process.

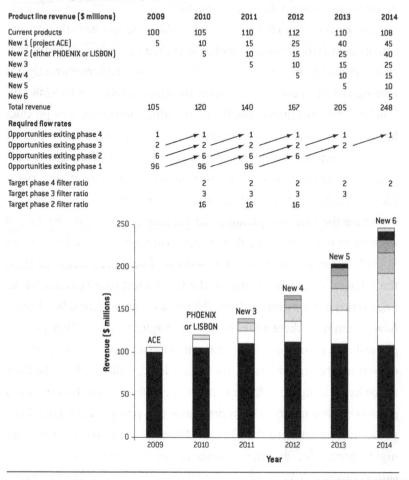

Product line revenue ($ millions)	2009	2010	2011	2012	2013	2014
Current products	100	105	110	112	110	108
New 1 (project ACE)	5	10	15	25	40	45
New 2 (either PHOENIX or LISBON)		5	10	15	25	40
New 3			5	10	15	25
New 4				5	10	15
New 5					5	10
New 6						5
Total revenue	105	120	140	167	205	248
Required flow rates						
Opportunities exiting phase 4	1	1	1	1	1	1
Opportunities exiting phase 3	2	2	2	2	2	
Opportunities exiting phase 2	6	6	6	6		
Opportunities exiting phase 1	96	96	96			
Target phase 4 filter ratio		2	2	2	2	2
Target phase 3 filter ratio		3	3	3	3	
Target phase 2 filter ratio		16	16	16		

SMOOTHING RESOURCE USE

The revenue pipeline is a top-down approach to planning. You can also take a bottom-up approach and examine the capacity of your resources and the demands imposed on them by opportunities under consideration. Pixar Animation Studios, creator of such hits as *Toy*

Story and *Finding Nemo*, begins its movie development process with oral presentations of ideas—"pitches," as they're known in the movie business—and then proceeds with selection and development of those ideas until a decision is made to animate a film, a commitment of more than $50 million (figure 7-6).[6]

Pixar's innovation process requires an expensive staff of professionals with deep expertise in areas such as writing, animation, and editing. Now, imagine that the executives at Pixar could choose between two scenarios relating to the future flow of opportunities as described in table 7-2. In both scenarios, Pixar would have, on average, two storyboards per animation and three animations per launch. Nevertheless, scenario 2 is less appealing. In some years, the specialists working on parts of the innovation process are flooded with work, whereas at other times they're largely idle. In 2008, they're juggling eight storyboards, yet in 2009 they have only four. Chances are that in 2008, some of the storyboards will face substantial delays, and in 2009 some creative people will have plenty of free time.

Corporate resources cannot always be adjusted quickly, so an uneven flow of opportunities (i.e., fluctuating resource requirements) causes mismatches in capacity and demand. That results in some combination of delays, stretching of capacity, or reduced quality.

The portfolio planning tool that helps you coordinate your resource needs is called the *resource stack*. Based on the data that you have prepared for the innovation pipeline (see previous section), you map

FIGURE 7-6

The innovation process at Pixar Animation Studios as of 2007.

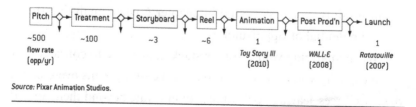

Source: Pixar Animation Studios.

TABLE 7-2

Two hypothetical scenarios describing the flow of opportunities at Pixar.

	SCENARIO 1			SCENARIO 2		
Year	Storyboards	Animations	Launch	Storyboards	Animations	Launch
2008	6	3	1	8	2	0
2009	6	3	1	4	3	1
2010	6	3	1	5	4	1
2011	6	3	1	7	3	2

out the work for each resource in the coming years. For example, a resource might be the rendering department of an animation studio. Figure 7-7 provides an example of how that department might be loaded with work corresponding to four new opportunities the company plans to exploit over the period 2008 to 2011 (i.e., features or short films). In 2008, for example, three opportunities require attention from the rendering department: opportunity 1 is winding down, opportunity 2 is consuming most of the available capacity, and opportunity 3 is nearing completion. The resource stack makes clear that in 2008 the requirements exceed the available capacity of the team, and so the company would have to either delay the development of an opportunity, take on a different mix of opportunities, add more capacity, engage an outside resource, or perform some combination of these actions.

The resource stack does not directly account for uncertainty. It is therefore more useful for resources required in the later phases of the development process, when probabilities of success for opportunities are relatively higher. In a more sophisticated version of the resource stack, you can use Monte Carlo simulation to understand the effects of uncertainty, much as we did in chapter 6 when analyzing the financial potential of opportunities.

When analyzing your resource stack, make sure to consider how much capacity you have for future projects. Many firms overcommit their resources, leaving no flexibility to innovate beyond their current

FIGURE 7-7

The resource stack helps a firm plan its capacity for developing opportunities in the future. This example is for a rendering department in an animation studio. A separate resource stack is created for each resource.

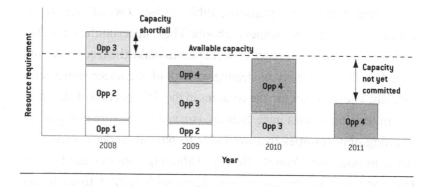

plans. But new opportunities will arise—they *should* arise if you're responsive to changes in your environment. Thus, as you look into the future, you should see more white space in your resource stack and fewer committed resources. The resource stack also forces you to reconcile your ambitions with the availability of resources. This reconciliation may force adjustments to one or the other.

HEDGING AGAINST EXTERNAL RISKS

Most firms are exposed to a great deal of uncertainty: zigzagging supply prices, unexpected moves by competitors, changes in the regulatory environment, and emerging-market booms and mature-market busts. By systemically making bets across a range of scenarios, you can prepare for the future, be it good or bad. When Toyota developed the Prius, with its gas-electric hybrid engine, the company took a bet on rising oil prices and global warming—a bet that looks a lot more prescient today than when Toyota placed it. Yet the company also prepared for a low oil-price future by maintaining a full line of burly SUVs and trucks. An ideal portfolio is one that is valuable across a broad range of scenarios. We refer to this as creating a robust innovation portfolio.

You can improve the robustness of your firm's innovation portfolio through *scenario planning*.[7] Scenario planning begins with a cataloging of major uncertainties. Table 7-3 lists a set of current uncertainties facing U.S. business schools. These uncertainties can then be bundled into a smaller set of scenarios to make them concrete and to reduce the complexity of dealing with all of the uncertainties individually. The scenarios are the columns in the right portion of the table.

In hedging against uncertainties, you want to ensure that you are selecting opportunities that are likely to pay off under a variety of different outcomes. You do this by evaluating your current lines of business and your current opportunities with respect to each scenario. Table 7-4 shows the four main lines of business for a business

TABLE 7-3

Scenario planning. To form scenarios, list major uncertainties and then group them.

	SCENARIOS			
Uncertainties	A *Status quo*	B *Price pressure*	C *New paradigm*	D *Foreign apps fall*
1. Online providers increasingly meet educational needs of students at low cost.		x	x	
2. U.S. foreign policy reduces the willingness of foreigners to come to the United States.				x
3. Stricter immigration laws restrict inflow of foreign students and faculty.				x
4. A major gift enables a key competitor to cut tuition by 50%.		x	x	
5. Strong regional competitors emerge in India and China.		x		x
6. Elite firms increasingly hire students out of college and train them internally instead of recruiting from MBA programs.		x		
7. Students increasingly resist traditional course-based approaches to education.			x	

TABLE 7-4

Payoff matrix. The payoff matrix evaluates the position of each product or service offering under each scenario. This helps to evaluate your organization's overall risk exposure.

	SCENARIOS			
Current businesses	A Status quo	B Price pressure	C New paradigm	D Foreign apps fall
Undergraduate	++	—	0	+
MBA	++	0	—	—
Doctoral program	++	+	0	0
Executive education	++	++	++	—
Opportunities				
Global executive MBA	—	—	0	+
Partner to offer MBA in China	—	+	0	+
Online continuing education venture	—	+	+	0
Learning technologies venture	0	0	+	0
Experiential learning experiments	0	—	++	0

++ represents very high payoffs; +, high payoffs; 0, median payoffs; and —, poor payoffs.

school, along with a set of opportunities. For each row, you subjectively rate the prospects for the current businesses and the opportunities under each scenario.

One does not need to be the dean of a business school to see the implications of the chart. The school is in a perfect position—if the future resembles the past. But the three alternative scenarios are likely to lead to a dramatic drop in performance. Of the five opportunities articulated, none is particularly promising if the status quo prevails. However, several of these opportunities become quite attractive if scenario B, C, or D unfolds. The opportunities to partner on an MBA in China, to explore an online continuing education venture, and to experiment with experiential learning provide insurance against the potentially devastating effects of scenario B, C, or D.

SUMMARY

The return curve assumes opportunities are independent of each other. Although it is a powerful tool, it fails to acknowledge the interdependencies among the opportunities.

We reviewed five ways in which opportunities are interdependent: market cannibalization, exploitation versus exploration, revenue smoothing, resource smoothing, and hedging against uncertainties. These five types of interdependencies and their associated portfolio tools fall into two broad categories:

⟹ **Balancing across time.** Just as the revenue pipeline aims to achieve smooth and steady growth, the resource stack helps to smooth capacity requirements. Strategic buckets strive for the same outcome but do so across longer time frames, namely, across the three uncertainty horizons. Smoothing helps you achieve a steady flow of innovation opportunities because you can't change your cost structure overnight.

⟹ **One plus one does not always make two.** When two opportunities target the same market segment, they typically earn less than they would have if they'd attacked separate segments. Partly, market cannibalization causes this. But you can also confront it when you attempt to prepare for different future scenarios. When facing higher oil prices, for example, lightweight vehicles might work as well as fuel cells. Yet once you decide to pursue one of these opportunities, the need and thus value of the other decreases. After all, you wouldn't buy two insurance policies on the same house. It is also possible that one plus one may make three. Pursuing two opportunities in the same category may benefit from synergies or efficiencies that could give rise to competitive advantage.

Diagnostics

➡ Have you categorized your opportunities by market segment? Which can be considered lead opportunities and which should be candidates for backups?

➡ Where do your product offerings stand in their life cycles? Do you have products in fast-growing markets, or are you primarily active in mature markets or markets that have not yet reached the growth phase? How much are you investing in exploration of new territory relative to exploitation of existing territory?

➡ Are the financial growth targets of your company linked to the development of your opportunities? Do you know how many opportunities you should be considering and developing at each phase of your innovation process to support your growth goals?

➡ At what time do you plan the resources requested from your innovation opportunities? Is your innovation pipeline congested (densely booked) or does it show white space in the future allowing you to have capacity for opportunities that you will create in the future?

➡ What are the biggest uncertainties in your industry? How well prepared are you in each of the resulting scenarios? Do you explicitly search for opportunities that could help you hedge a weak position?

LONG-TERM PROFITABILITY

Managing Far-Horizon Opportunities

Segway introduced its personal transporter (figure 8-1) with great fanfare in 2000. The entrepreneur leading Segway, Dean Kamen, planned for his company to make 40,000 units per month by the end of the company's first full year of production.[1] At prices exceeding $5,000 per unit, this would amount to annual sales of more than $2.5 billion. Dreams of this kind of fortune enticed a prominent venture capitalist, John Doerr of Kleiner Perkins Caufield & Byers, to lead an investment syndicate that bet $80 million on Kamen's company.[2] Segway was a far-horizon opportunity for Kamen and his investors, representing the application of a new technology to an emerging market for light-duty, battery-powered personal transportation devices. But after *five years*, Segway had sold 23,000 units—about *two weeks'* worth of the demand that Kamen had originally forecast.[3]

Segway's failure to achieve widespread consumer acceptance as forecast isn't unusual. Indeed, the probability of success for a far-horizon innovation is quite low; when you're operating at innovation's frontiers,

FIGURE 8-1

The Segway scooter is a two-wheeled, electric-powered personal mobility device.

Source: Wikipedia.

big risks will always dog you. The question for an innovator isn't how to preclude them. Rather, it's which ones you should take and how to maximize your chances of success while minimizing the costs of failure.

Chapter 4 divided the technology–market map into three zones of opportunities: horizons 1, 2, and 3 (figure 8-2). Managing near-horizon opportunities differs from managing far-horizon ones. Far-horizon opportunities are unavoidably risky. By definition, they represent leaps into the unknown.

DEFINING YOUR INNOVATION FRONTIER

The innovation frontier for a particular company is the boundary of the technology–market map beyond which you choose not to pursue opportunities (figure 8-3). Defining your frontier forces you to think

FIGURE 8-2

Three horizons for opportunities based on the extent to which the technology and market are known.

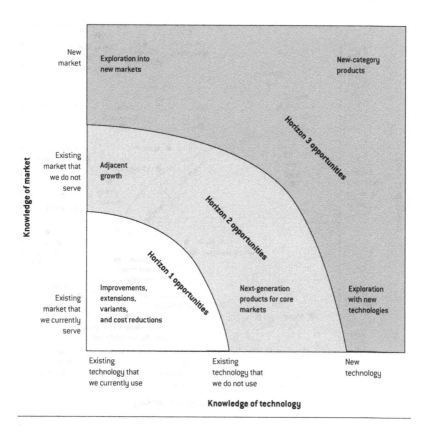

carefully about your capabilities and strategy. Some far-horizon opportunities involve new-to-the-world technologies and markets, including such once-radical innovations as television, the phonograph, and heavier-than-air flight. But for most firms, far-horizon opportunities are not as dramatically new as Edison's phonograph. For example, W. L. Gore applied its expertise in producing expanded polytetrafluoroethylene to the need for a dental floss that didn't shred when used with tightly spaced teeth. This was an opportunity on the far horizon for Gore but hardly comparable to the Wright brothers' work at Kitty Hawk. Indeed, most innovation for established firms will occur close to existing markets and technologies.

FIGURE 8-3

Existing firms face decisions about how to define the innovation frontier; that is, the amount of uncertainty they will take on in exploring opportunities.

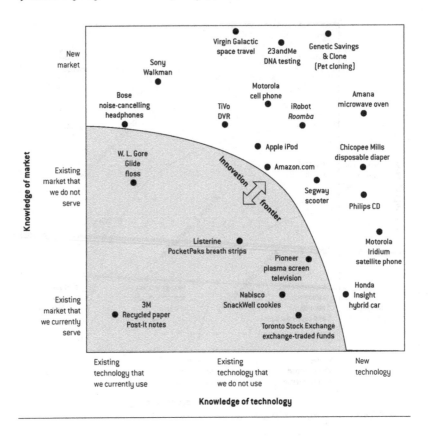

A chorus of writers and consultants admonishes established firms to invest in opportunities on the distant horizon. We're more equivocal in our recommendations. We don't believe that that's the right strategy for everyone. Consider the history of some highly successful innovations resulting from far-horizon opportunities, as shown in table 8-1.[4] A couple of patterns stand out in the chart. First, the firms that first achieve success (labeled "first mainstream product") usually lag the pioneers by quite a few years. In one case, the delay was only a year (in search engines), but in several cases, it was more than a decade (e.g., for video recorders). Second, companies that lead a category during the booming growth period are rarely the pioneers.[5] Google,

TABLE 8-1

The pioneers and eventual leaders for several new-category innovations.

Innovation	Early commercial attempts	First mainstream product	Leader(s) during peak growth period
Cable television	Panther Valley Cable TV, Service Electric Cable TV 1948	Cox, Westinghouse, Teleprompter ~1960	Comcast, Time Warner, Cox, TCI, Cablevision, MediaOne ~1985
Compact fluorescent light bulb	Philips, Westinghouse ~1980	Philips, Westinghouse, GE ~1985	Philips, GE, Westinghouse, N:Vision, Sylvania ~1990
Disposable diapers	PauliStrom 1942	Chicopee Mills (J&J) 1949	Procter & Gamble, Kimberly Clark 1961
Microwave oven	Raytheon 1947	Amana (Raytheon) 1967	Litton ~1970
Mobile telephone	Motorola 1973	Motorola 1983	Nokia, Motorola ~1991
Mutual fund	Massachusetts Investors Trust 1924	Fidelity Fund 1928	Vanguard Group Fidelity Investments 1977
Personal computer	MITS Altair 1975	Apple II 1977	IBM PC 1985
Search engine	Lycos 1994	Excite, AltaVista, Yahoo! 1995	Google, 1998 Yahoo!, Microsoft, 2004
Television	Telefunken, 1934 Dumont, 1938	RCA 1948	Magnavox, Zenith, Philips ~1960
Video cassette recorder	Ampex 1956	Sony 1971	Matsushita 1976

Sources: Peter Golder and Gerard Tellis, "Will It Ever Fly? Modeling the Takeoff of Really New Consumer Durables," *Marketing Science* 16, no. 3 (1997); Rajshree Agarwal and Barry Bayus, "The Market Evolution and Sales Takeoff of Product Innovations," *Management Science* 48, no. 8 (2002); and authors' research.

for example, dominates the market for Internet search in 2009, but Lycos pioneered it. Vanguard and Fidelity lead the mutual fund business, but Massachusetts Investors Trust first entered the market.

The historical evidence is sobering enough that we believe the right strategy for some firms may be to shun far-horizon opportunities. Let other companies explore the far horizon, and then you can follow them, or even try to acquire them, once they've proved the opportunity. Among the issues to consider as you define your innovation frontier are the following, all but the last of which are cautions against pioneering the far horizon.

➡ **Irrational entry in emerging markets.** As new markets emerge, many firms enter, but few survive. This behavior may reflect overly optimistic expectations and herdlike behavior. Either way, excess entry reduces the profit potential for pioneers.[6]

➡ **First-mover advantages.** Despite conventional wisdom to the contrary, research suggests that first movers usually do not dominate their markets. In theory, the first mover can develop expertise, lock down access to scarce assets, and benefit from the stickiness of customer tastes. However, a first mover also effectively tests markets and technologies in public. It must bear the greatest burden of educating consumers, while potential rivals watch from the sidelines.[7]

➡ **Viability of near-horizon strategies.** Many successful firms grow and increase profits without engaging in substantial far-horizon innovation.[8] Microsoft may be the most prominent example. Most of its revenues and profits come from products and services that followed other firms' innovations. Microsoft Windows was built on pioneering efforts by Xerox, Apple, and others. Microsoft Office was built on the pioneering efforts by WordPerfect, Visicalc, Lotus, Aldus, and others.

➡ **Capabilities for exploration and exploitation.** The capabilities required for successful exploration and development of new markets differ from those needed to exploit established ones.[9] Few firms excel at both.[10] Chapter 10 addresses the challenge of accommodating both approaches in the same organization.

➡ **Absorptive capacity.** It's easy to say you'll wait and see which far-horizon opportunities pan out and then scurry into those markets, swiping share from the pioneers. But this strategy requires an ability to evaluate technologies in a new market, and that ability—also called *absorptive capacity*—resembles the skills required to develop opportunities within a firm.[11] Therefore, one reason to engage in exploration of far-horizon opportunities is to develop the capacity to evaluate and absorb technologies.

We can't give you unambiguous prescriptions about how far-reaching your innovation frontier should be. Determining that requires judgment and firm-specific knowledge. But whatever decision you make, make it deliberately, after considering the five issues just discussed.

STRUCTURING TASKS FOR FAR-HORIZON INNOVATION

The very nature of innovation tournaments dictates that you'll abandon most far-horizon innovation projects. In a sense, timely abandonment should be a goal of your innovation process for these kinds of opportunities. You should aim to spend as little as possible to learn enough so that you can decide whether to ditch an opportunity or, more rarely, invest further. We'll repeat the mantra from chapter 6: fail often, fail early, and fail inexpensively. Our method for structuring development tasks for far-horizon opportunities has three steps:

1. List the major tasks required before the opportunity can be commercialized, and estimate their cost and their effect on uncertainty.

2. Construct a sequence of tasks that both efficiently reduces uncertainty and sensibly orders tasks that must be completed.

3. If you need to move fast, consider completing some tasks in parallel instead of sequentially.

List Tasks

You should attempt to list a set of tasks that answer key questions and therefore resolve critical uncertainties. Ideally, you will limit this list to about five to fifteen major challenges, which will allow you to think clearly about the sequence in which you should address the tasks.[12] Table 8-2 is a list of tasks and the questions that Segway might have addressed when it embarked on developing the opportunity to apply its dynamic stabilization technology to personal transportation. The table lists each task, its effect on uncertainty, and its estimated cost. The effect on uncertainty is ranked, subjectively, on a scale of 1 to 5. Completing the alpha prototype, for example, could answer the question of the acceptability of the product's technical

TABLE 8-2

A set of tasks that could reduce the uncertainty of Segway's innovation opportunity. For each task, the potential relative effect on uncertainty is shown on a scale of 1 to 5, with 5 representing the greatest reduction in uncertainty.

Task	Questions addressed	Potential reduction in uncertainty	Cost of task ($ millions)
A Complete alpha prototype design, fabrication, and testing.	Will the technical performance of the product be acceptable?	••••	1
B Complete production-intent design, engineering refinement, and life testing.	How reliable and robust can we make the product?	•	5
C Design supply chain and set up production facility.	Can we establish production capacity?	•	3
D Lobby for new legislation in state and local governments.	In how many states will it be legal to ride on the streets and sidewalks?	•••	7
E File patents.	What is the extent of the intellectual property barrier?	••	0.10
F Recruit full management team of new company.	Can we establish the structure and personnel to support a large enterprise?	•	1 (+0.5/month)
G Conduct customer interviews and demonstrations.	Which market segments will most resonate with the benefits of the product? What is the core benefit proposition for the product? Where will the user ride the product?	•••••	0.10
H Perform competitive product analysis, customer surveys, and retailer surveys.	What should be the target price point?	•••	0.05
I Complete diffusion modeling, historical comparisons, and purchase intent survey.	What is likely to be the sales trajectory?	••••	0.10

performance, which was a major uncertainty for Segway. Likewise, designing and organizing the supply chain could determine whether the venture could achieve sufficient production capacity.

Construct a Feasible and Efficient Task Sequence

In most cases the best task sequence reduces the most uncertainty at the lowest cost. Given the low odds of success for a far-horizon opportunity, such a sequence allows you to abandon an opportunity before making most of the investment (that is, it lets you fail inexpensively). Understand, however, that not all task sequences work. You typically cannot construct a good sales forecast without having collected some survey data, and you cannot organize your supply chain if you have not first designed your product. Limitations on the order in which tasks can be completed are shown in figure 8-4, an approach called a *precedence diagram*. The diagram shows, for example, that the prototype (task A) must be done before the demonstrations, survey, and forecast (tasks G, H, and I) can be. Other tools, such as the design structure matrix and PERT charts, offer more sophisticated ways to map task structure, but for most far-horizon projects, the level of detail in figure 8-4 suffices.[13]

Once you understand your task dependencies, you can create a sequence that is efficient and feasible. Two task sequences appear in figure 8-5. The upper sequence—approximately the one that Segway pursued—shows that expensive tasks lacking dramatic impact on uncertainty were completed early. An alternative sequence appears below it. In this one, tasks are completed in an order that dramatically reduces uncertainty at a fraction of the cost. In both, the first task is making a prototype, which must be completed before many others. Doing so reduces a lot of uncertainty at modest cost. But the alternative sequence then deviates. Instead of charging ahead with the full production-intent engineering of the product and design and implementation of the supply chain, Segway could have done market research, including demonstrations, surveys, and sales forecasting.

FIGURE 8-4

The dependencies among tasks for the Segway opportunity. The cost for each task
(in millions) and its effect on uncertainty (the more dots, the greater the reduction in
uncertainty) appear below each task label.

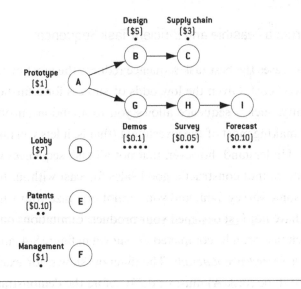

FIGURE 8-5

Investment in innovation tasks should reduce uncertainty. However, the rate at which uncertainty is reduced is determined by the sequence of tasks. This graphic plots the uncertainty
reduction, as represented by the dots in table 8-2, as a function of cumulative investment.

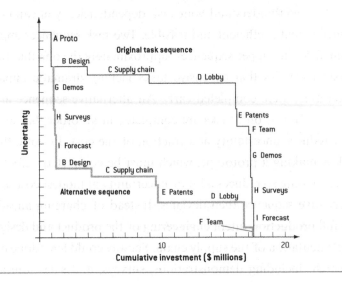

These tasks are cheap but reduce a lot of uncertainty. The alternative sequence might have led to a decision to abandon the opportunity, or more likely, to redirect the development effort. This task sequence could have therefore prevented wasteful investment in, for example, establishing a high-volume supply chain inappropriate for the opportunity.

Consider Parallel Tasks to Increase Speed, If Appropriate

An argument against a deliberate, carefully staged approach to far-horizon innovation is that competitors will beat you to the market. This fear has little justification in reality. On average, pioneering firms in new categories do not become the long-term profit leaders.[14] We are not saying that getting to market is never urgent. In some industries, like fashion, market windows open only briefly. In others, players can avail themselves of opportunities for "land grabs," as happened with Internet domain-name hoarding. But most time-critical innovation projects are not far-horizon opportunities.

If unusual circumstances do call for a reduction of development time, some tasks can be completed in parallel. For example, tasks D, E, and F in table 8-2—lobbying, patents, and creating a management team—can be undertaken at any time because they do not depend substantially on the other tasks. Overlapping these tasks will clearly save time. The potential downside is that costs will be incurred even if the opportunity ends up being abandoned based on evidence from the completion of the design and supply-chain tasks.

PITFALLS IN FAR-HORIZON INNOVATION

As we've discussed, far-horizon innovation is unavoidably risky. Sometimes, however, innovators redouble their risks by making common mistakes. Two of these are so typical and avoidable that they deserve special attention: violating the *what-not-how principle* and overestimating diffusion rates for new-category products.

The What-Not-How Principle

Remember that we defined innovation as a new match between a solution and a need. Successful innovation adds value, meaning that the user will pay more for the solution than the cost of delivering it. But just because a solution meets a need does not mean that the innovator can extract value from it. The solution must cost-efficiently meet the need. Otherwise, the innovator probably won't make any money from it.

Let's look again at Segway. Its scooters aim to provide personal transportation over distances of less than a few miles. A Segway scooter successfully meets this need, particularly in pedestrian environments like city sidewalks, airports, and warehouses. But that does not mean that Segway's innovation creates value. Meeting a need is a *necessary* condition for value creation but not a *sufficient* one.

The other condition required is that the solution be cost-efficient. A Segway scooter costs more than $5,000. As of this writing, that's twice the projected price of the entry-level *automobile* Tata Motors is developing for the Indian market. A Segway is expensive because its dynamic-stabilization technology requires two motors, two sets of drive electronics, several sophisticated position sensors, and a high level of fault tolerance. Yet in only a few instances does a dynamically stabilized scooter beat a simpler one with a single motor and a simple throttle. Indeed, in Segway's niche, competing products, using simpler technologies, cost far less (figure 8-6). What's more, walking or biking often trump a Segway, too.

Segway assumed from the outset that it would introduce a particular solution—a *how*—and then went looking for a need that its solution could address. This pitfall is sometimes called *technology push*. Instead of asking "*How* can we employ two-wheeled dynamic-stabilization technology?" Segway might have asked "*What* would provide efficient personal transportation for city dwellers?" Starting with the what, not the how, leaves open a universe of solutions in which a value-creating innovation can be discovered.

FIGURE 8-6

The Rad2Go Q Transporter applies a different solution to the same need addressed by the Segway. Its trailing wheels forestall the need for dynamic stabilization, lowering its price to about $1,000.

Source: Rad2Go.

The what-not-how principle almost always holds. But a few settings, including pharmaceuticals and basic materials, exist in which technology push prevails. In these industries, innovators often begin with chemical compounds and try to discover uses for them. This process is inefficient but unavoidable. Innovators in these fields do not yet possess the scientific know-how and the synthesis methods to allow them to begin with an unmet need and create a chemical compound to address it. Such an approach remains the Holy Grail in the drug industry and would allow compliance even there with the what-not-how principle.

Diffusion Rates for Far-Horizon Innovation

A few years ago, we were driving to visit a company with one of our doctoral students, newly arrived in the United States from India. As we passed quickly through a tollbooth thanks to the EZ Pass automated toll-collection system, he stared at the long lines of cars at the cash-only booths and wondered, "Why doesn't everybody have EZ

Pass?" The EZ Pass system (and its equivalents in other places) offers a clear, compelling benefit, and yet it took six years to reach a 30 percent share of toll transactions on the New York State Thruway, where it was introduced.[15] That's not unusual. In fact, EZ Pass is considered a phenomenal success. The normal time required for far-horizon innovation to diffuse is astoundingly long. A pitfall for ever-optimistic innovators is to believe that your innovation will somehow differ.

But virtually all successful innovations follow a similar pattern of diffusion, illustrated by the examples of the Web browser and the mobile telephone in figure 8-7. Adoption starts slowly, proceeds through a period of relatively rapid growth, and then slows considerably as the market becomes saturated. Different innovations, however, exhibit markedly different lags between launch and "takeoff" and different growth rates at their peak. Understand, too, that these are the patterns exhibited by innovations *eventually accepted* by consumers. Plenty of innovations never take off at all.

FIGURE 8-7

Adoption of innovation follows an S-curve pattern reflecting incubation, rapid growth, and finally saturation. These curves are approximations based on data from a variety of sources.

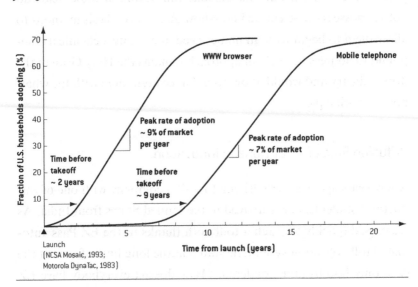

For far-horizon innovation, we can find no instances of takeoff starting in less than about two years. Most take much longer. Mutual funds, introduced to the public in 1924, didn't really take off until the 1980s. Many scholars have studied this phenomenon, and the sociologist Everett Rogers has shown that five variables substantially explain the rate at which consumers adopt innovations.[16]

➡ **Relative advantage.** How much better is the innovation than alternatives already in use? Innovations that offer huge advantages are more likely to spur action than those that offer slight ones. Advantages usually improve with time as costs fall and performance improves.

➡ **Visibility.** How readily can reluctant consumers see early adopters using the innovation? Information drives adoption, and the rate at which it travels depends in part on the ability to observe the behavior of others.

➡ **Trialability.** Can a potential adopter try the product without sacrificing much time, effort, and money? Trials resolve uncertainty and reduce risk for potential adopters. The easier trial is, the more readily an innovation will diffuse.

➡ **Simplicity.**[17] Is the function and use of the innovation obvious? Are the benefits readily apparent?

➡ **Compatibility.** Does the innovation require adopters to change other elements of their lives, or can the innovation be adopted as a single, independent action?

Table 8-3 shows how these factors can be evaluated for a sample of innovations. In this case, we subjectively assess on a 1-to-5 scale the relative value of the five drivers of diffusion. You can do this sort of evaluation before launching an innovation, or even before making a substantial investment in one. With your evaluation in hand, you can predict how your diffusion rate will likely compare with that of other far-horizon innovations. As you do this, bear in mind that two

TABLE 8-3

Comparison of the five factors driving diffusion rates for several far-horizon opportunities.

	EZ Pass auto toll system	Web browser	Mobile phone	Segway personal transporter
Relative advantage	••••• No waiting at toll booths	••••• Free, instant information	•••• Wireless calling, but initially expensive	• Better than walking?
Visibility	••••• Obvious to all users	• Not very visible	•••• Visible in public	••••• Highly visible
Trialability	•• Must enroll to try	••••• Free download	•• Contract required	• $10 K commitment
Simplicity	••• How does payment work? Who installs?	••••• Click and view	•• "Send" button? Reception, coverage?	•• How does that thing work? What powers it?
Compatibility	••••• All vehicles	••••• All PCs	••••• Fits in pocket or bag	•• Storage? Locking? Where to ride? Charging?
Predicted relative rate	Fast	Very fast	Moderate	Very slow
Years to takeoff	~3	~2	~9	8 and counting...

years is an extraordinarily short takeoff time and that many innovations require five to ten years of incubation before takeoff.

SUMMARY

Managing near-horizon opportunities differs from undertaking far-horizon ones. Far-horizon opportunities are unavoidably risky. They represent leaps into the unknown. A key strategic decision that you'll face as an innovator is the extent to which your innovation frontier explores new categories of products and services. Not all firms must pursue far-horizon opportunities.

Given that most far-horizon opportunities will not prove worthy of commercialization, the goal of managing far-horizon opportunities is to reduce as much uncertainty as possible with as little investment as possible. This goal can be achieved through an analysis of the structure of the tasks required to pursue an opportunity.

Two pitfalls in far-horizon innovation are (1) violation of the what-not-how principle and (2) overestimating the rate of adoption of far-horizon innovations. With awareness of the pitfalls you can avoid them.

Diagnostics

→ How far out does your innovation frontier currently extend? How carefully have you considered the five issues that determine the extent of your frontier?

→ Do you determine the sequence in which you address innovation tasks in order to reduce uncertainty in the most efficient fashion?

→ Which opportunities that you are pursuing violate the what-not-how principle?

→ How can you ensure that the solutions you are developing will result in value creation?

→ What are you assuming for adoption rates of your far-horizon opportunities? Would you expect these diffusion rates based on the factors developed in this chapter?

STRUCTURE

Shaping the Innovation Funnel

A pharmaceutical company considers, on average, about ten thousand newly discovered chemical compounds for every drug it introduces. A movie studio will consider two hundred to five hundred script summaries for every film it produces. These daunting ratios are illustrated in figure 9-1.

We have noted already that organizations use tournaments to winnow many opportunities down to the exceptional few that can become profitable innovations. The basic tournament structure used in virtually all organizations is a sequence of development tasks punctuated by filters that separate winners and losers. This structure is illustrated by figure 9-2. This diagram reflects some of the complexity of real tournaments in that new opportunities spring up in the middle of the process, and one opportunity can spawn others.

Corporate innovators, whether they're creating movies or molecules, often refer to their collection of opportunities, ranging from

FIGURE 9-1

Pharmaceutical companies evaluate about ten thousand newly discovered chemical compounds for every new drug introduced. Movie studios typically consider two hundred to five hundred script summaries for every film produced.

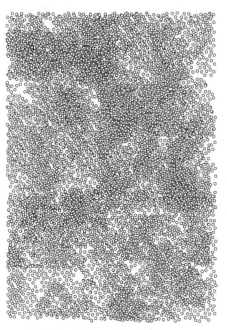

8–12 years
$500 million–$1 billion

1 new drug

10,000 newly discovered compounds

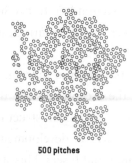

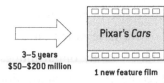

3–5 years
$50–$200 million

1 new feature film

500 pitches

FIGURE 9-2

A series of tasks and filters are used to winnow myriad raw opportunities down to a few exceptional ones.

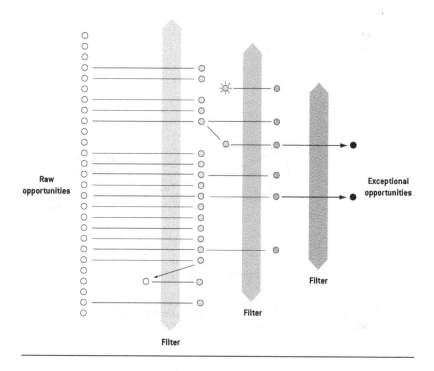

newly conceived ideas to products and services nearly ready for market, as a *pipeline,* or they call the tournament process a *funnel,* emphasizing the fact that the entrance to the process is in a sense "wide" while the exit is "narrow." (Note that neither of these metaphors works perfectly. Whatever goes into pipelines and funnels gushes out, which is not true of innovation processes.)

Figure 9-3 shows the shapes of the funnels in several different industries, with the number of opportunities considered at each phase of the innovation process relative to a single launch in the marketplace. Note the variation in funnels across different industries and even within industries. As you consider the shape of your company's funnel, you should ask at least three questions. First, how wide should its mouth be? That is, how many raw opportunities should be

FIGURE 9-3

The number of opportunities considered at each phase for each innovation that is eventually launched.

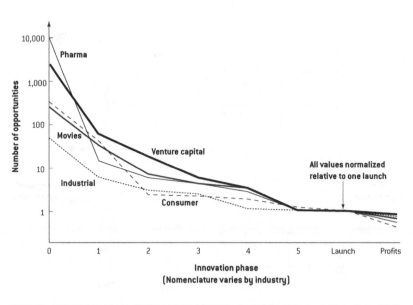

Sources: One paper that does a nice job of laying out the basic idea in the diagram is Greg A. Stevens and James Burley, "3000 Ideas = 1 Commercial Success," *Research-Technology Management*, May–June 1997, 16–27. The data for the pharmaceutical industry are from Paraxel's *Bio/Pharmaceutical R&D Statistical Sourcebook, 2002/2003* (Waltham, MA).

considered for every innovation launched in the market? Second, how aggressively should the neck of the funnel be tapered—should raw opportunities be filtered immediately or should many be allowed to survive through several rounds? Third, to what extent should innovation tournaments be run as pure cascades, with opportunities flowing strictly in one direction, as opposed to whirlpools, in which opportunities can flow back upstream and be transformed into improved versions? This chapter tackles these questions.

SIZING THE MOUTH OF THE FUNNEL

On first glance, the question of how big the mouth of the funnel should be is easy. The rough size of the mouth of the innovation pipeline is determined by the average quality of the raw material that flows into the pipeline. Because 9,999 of 10,000 newly discovered chemical compounds are either biologically inert or toxic, pharmaceutical firms have to examine more than 10,000 compounds on average to find one that will become a drug. Because a movie studio can find a feasible film, at best, once in every two hundred script summaries, it needs to consider a minimum of two hundred ideas. The fifty-fold difference in the size of the mouths of these two funnels is explained by the fifty-fold difference in the average probability of success in these industries. But a more subtle question lurks here, too. As a pharmaceutical company, should you perhaps consider 12,000 compounds instead of 10,000? As a movie studio, should you consider three hundred script summaries instead of two hundred? In other words, once the pipeline is sized according to an industry's typical probabilities, should you be considering more or fewer opportunities than average?

Widening the mouth corresponds to moving from top to bottom in figure 9-4; the process achieves the same rate of commercialized innovations from more opportunities. All else being equal, this action increases the average value of the firm's innovations. The *quantity* of launches does not increase, but their average *quality* does. By considering more feature film pitches, Pixar, for example, will increase the average quality of each film it releases. Coming in first in a race of five hundred is simply a bigger accomplishment than coming in first in a race of two hundred.

But just because you *can* do something doesn't mean that you *should*. Widening the mouth of the funnel costs money, and the outlay may exceed the added value that you get from considering more opportunities. Three factors should inform your decision regarding whether to widen: the cost of generating and screening opportunities, the variance in the quality of your opportunities, and the importance of their quality in determining the value of the launched innovation. We'll consider each of these in turn. But before we do, we'd be remiss if we didn't point out that in almost all settings that we have encountered, *the mouth of the funnel should be widened*. So

FIGURE 9-4

Two structures for an innovation tournament. The tournament on the bottom considers about 50 percent more raw opportunities for the same number of exceptional ones pursued.

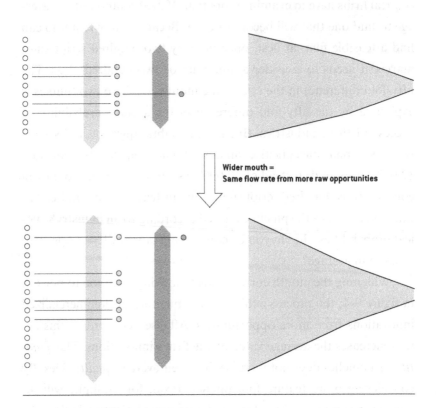

Wider mouth =
Same flow rate from more raw opportunities

although we'll explain the economics behind this belief, we want to emphasize that the decision to widen the funnel does not typically rely on subtle analysis. You will almost certainly benefit if you "just do it."

Cost of Generating and Screening Opportunities

The lower the cost of generating and screening opportunities, the greater the number that you should consider. If generating and screening opportunities cost little and consumed insignificant time, you would consider millions of alternatives before selecting an exceptional opportunity. Conversely, if generating and screening an opportunity cost a lot and took years, you would consider only a few. Fortunately, in the early phases of the innovation process, generation and screening are typically relatively cheap, often only a few dollars to a few thousand dollars per raw opportunity. Let's consider some examples.

- **Product and brand names.** At the low end of the cost scale are product and brand names. People skilled at the task can conceive more than fifty names per hour, resulting in costs of just a few dollars per name.

- **New products and services.** We have run many workshops focused on generating and screening opportunities for new products and services, in industries ranging from candy to consulting. In a typical workshop, about twenty professionals work for one day and generate and screen about two hundred opportunities. If you value their time at about $2,000 per day, then these opportunities cost about $200 each to generate and screen. We have done these calculations in a variety of settings and consistently find costs in the range of $50 to $500 per raw opportunity. These figures are also consistent with the fees charged by consulting firms to generate and screen opportunities.

- **Entertainment.** The *American Idol* television competition (and its variants in countries other than the United States) provides some evidence of the costs of identifying talent—that is, raw opportunities—in the music industry. The staff of the show tours about half a dozen cities, auditioning about 100,000 singers. They filter the candidates in three rounds, narrowing the field to between 100 and 200 candidates who travel to Hollywood for subsequent auditions. If the cost of handling and evaluating these 100,000 wannabe stars is between $20 million and $30 million, including the considerable cost of the celebrity judges, then potential new artists cost $200 to $300 each to identify and screen.

→ **Pharmaceuticals.** A sample of a new chemical compound, often extracted from soil samples collected in nature, costs less than $100. Screening each compound against a set of known biological targets costs from $1,000 to $5,000. Even if ten thousand compounds must be screened for every new product, these costs are not very high relative to the value of a blockbuster drug.

Variance in Quality of Opportunities

Recall that in chapter 1 we argued that the opportunity generation process is not like a typical production process, for which you seek to minimize variation. As an innovator, you benefit from increased variation in the quality of your raw opportunities because you are seeking a few exceptional ones, not many that are simply satisfactory.

As far as we know, the role of variance in the quality of opportunities has until very recently been only a theoretical concept.[1] To probe it, we have analyzed data gathered during the process of generating opportunities for new ventures. Recall from chapter 2 that we studied opportunities identified by a group of forty-seven managers in the Wharton School's executive MBA program who cooperated to create a new business. The executives, with an average of about ten years of work experience, typified the educated innovators who attempt to create valuable new enterprises. We asked each one to identify about five unique opportunities and submit them via the Darwinator, our Web-based tool for evaluating and analyzing concepts. (The Darwinator software is described in more detail in chapter 4 and is available for use by readers of this book at www.InnovationTournaments .com.) The executives also each evaluated, on a scale of 1 to 10, about 100 opportunities submitted by their classmates. The Darwinator averaged these evaluations and ranked the opportunities accordingly. We ended up with a sample of 234 opportunities, each rated by twenty peers. Figure 9-5 shows a histogram of the estimated quality of the 234 opportunities. Based on this distribution, we see that highly rated opportunities are truly exceptional; the executives identified many middling opportunities for every exceptionally good one.

Imagine that instead of generating many ideas, this group had generated and considered only *one*. How good would it be? If it were statistically average, you would expect it to be about a "5.5" idea from figure 9-5. What if you were to generate another opportunity? How good would the *better* of these two opportunities be? You would expect the best of two ideas drawn from the distribution in figure 9-5 to be better than if you just drew one, perhaps rating about 6 of 10, a significant improvement. The more opportunities you identify, the better the quality of the best of those identified. Yet the rate

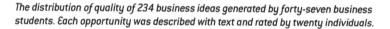

FIGURE 9-5

The distribution of quality of 234 business ideas generated by forty-seven business students. Each opportunity was described with text and rated by twenty individuals.

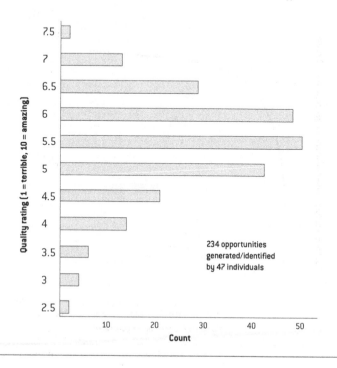

at which you see improvement diminishes as you identify more of them. This idea is illustrated in figure 9-6.

The variance in the quality of ideas—that is, the "spread" in the distribution in figure 9-5—determines the shape of the curve in figure 9-6. The more spread out the distribution of ideas, the greater the impact that generating another idea will have on the quality of the best one. Like their counterparts in the world of finance, innovation options are more valuable when their underlying "price" is volatile.

As a practical matter, if the quality of your opportunities varies widely, then you'll benefit from considering more. *American Idol* contestants vary tremendously in their singing ability. The auditions

FIGURE 9-6

The quality of the best opportunity, as a function of the number of opportunities identified. These specific values are for a specific industry context. Although the shape of this curve is likely to be similar across industries, the values may be different.

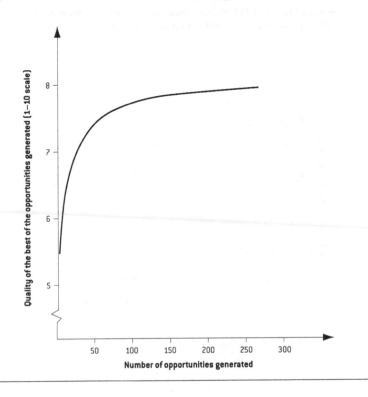

evaluate about 100,000 of them in an attempt to find a star. Consider, in contrast, a process of selecting a parking lot attendant. Although there may be some who are better than others at this task, the range of skills in the candidate pool relative to this task does not vary as much as for singing. As a result, you would need to evaluate just a handful of candidates to find the one you hire.

How Much Does a Good Opportunity Matter in Determining Value?

If the raw opportunity contributes mightily to the value of the innovation, then finding a good one matters a lot, and you should consider more. But if almost any notion can be turned into a valuable innovation with the right development activities, then the raw opportunity may matter less than the quality of the development process. Obviously, a good idea is more valuable than a bad one. But how much more valuable is, say, an "8 of 10" than a 7.5? Here are some anecdotal insights.

Merck's drug Zocor and Pixar's movie *Cars* show how greatly the value of ideas can differ. With Zocor, the raw opportunity was the chemical compound simvastatin ($C_{25}H_{38}O_5$). For Merck, all the value of Zocor springs from its biological properties, which were present in the compound even before Merck's researchers discovered it. Nothing Merck does can change the intrinsic properties of $C_{25}H_{38}O_5$. It is what it is. Furthermore, because this compound addressed a large unmet medical need (reducing blood cholesterol), it was fantastically more valuable than if it provided a slight incremental improvement to an existing treatment for dandruff.

For Pixar's movie *Cars*, the raw opportunity was a one-sentence story summary that went something like this: a hot-shot race car named Lightning McQueen gets waylaid in Radiator Springs, where he finds the true meaning of friendship and family. In this case, the idea matters, but a huge portion of Pixar's magic comes from its scripts, animation, music, voices, and direction. Pixar wants a compelling story, but its success doesn't hinge on one. Pixar can probably turn a sub-par story into a movie that will thrive at the box office if combined with an outstanding cast, writer, and director. For Merck, a great molecule could provide ten times the profits of a merely good one. For Pixar, a great story idea won't result in a movie that earns ten times the profit of a movie based on a merely good idea.

Integrating the Factors to Size the Mouth of the Funnel

With that as background, let's return to the question of how many opportunities you should consider. To answer it, you have to weigh the costs and benefits of increasing the size of the mouth of your funnel. To this end, you must answer three questions:

1. How much would it cost to generate and evaluate twice as many raw opportunities?

2. What is the difference in economic value in your industry between an average innovation and a top 10 percent innovation? If there are a substantial number of innovations in an industry, as in the movie business, it is easy to compare the return for an average innovation with that of the top 10 percent of innovations. If you work in an industry for which little data exist, you will probably be best off estimating this difference in value based on the judgments of several experts.

3. How critical is the quality of the raw opportunity in determining economic value in your industry? In answering, consider whether your industry resembles the movie business or the pharmaceutical business in terms of the importance of the intrinsic properties of the raw opportunity. One factor that contributes to the importance of the opportunity itself is how quickly and easily an innovation can be copied by a competitor. If the intellectual property associated with the raw opportunity can be tightly protected, then the opportunity can be quite important.

Once you've answered these questions, you can subjectively judge whether you should be considering more raw opportunities. As we said earlier, the answer is almost always that you should consider more.

To see this in action, consider the case of a maker of commercial heating, ventilation, and cooling products. The company's business development team normally considers about fifty ideas per year for new products and services. The team could double the number of opportunities it considers by running one workshop and by actively soliciting ideas from employees, and the cost would be a total of about $50,000. Based on historical evidence, the company's average new product or service contributes about $12 million in net present value, and the standard deviation of the value of new offerings is also about $12 million. For this company, the raw opportunity dictates the size and growth of the market for the new offering, which determines a substantial part of the economic value of the innovation. The raw opportunity largely determines whether the innovation results in $12 million in value or $24 million or more. The calculation of these values suggests that doubling the number of raw opportunities considered would need to only shift the profit potential of a single innovation by less than 0.5 percent of a standard deviation to justify the cost. Here, the potential benefits are so much larger than the costs that a more sophisticated analysis isn't needed.

Economists reading this may object to our logic on two grounds. First, they may say that if it were so easy to increase profit potential, then firms would already be doing it. (This is analogous to the old joke that an economist will tell you that there can't possibly be a $100 bill on the ground because, if it were there, someone would have already picked it up.) Second, they may argue that, at some point, the number of opportunities swells to the point at which generating more does not add value, and you may already have reached that point. Both of these arguments are valid in theory and could eventually become important in practice. We, however, believe strongly that, with innovation management still in its infancy, opportunities abound to dramatically improve performance for most firms.

SHAPING THE NECK OF THE FUNNEL

If you could reliably pick a winner from the available raw opportunities, your innovation funnel would start wide and then narrow to a single opportunity at the first filter, looking like the tournament in figure 9-7. This would be a happy state of affairs, allowing you to save the trouble and expense of pursuing more than one opportunity through multiple phases of development.

Ponder, however, some data from an innovation tournament that we conducted. Figure 9-8 shows the fate of about fifty raw opportunities as they moved through three phases of the tournament. The first phase culminated with a brief pitch; the second, with a more detailed concept pitch; and the third, with the presentation of a full-fledged business plan. At the end of each stage, a group of fifty raters scored each opportunity. In the figure, we've arranged the opportunities vertically according to these quality scores. The raters filtered the opportunities based on both the quality scores and on the enthusiasm of teams to carry an opportunity forward, which is why some of

FIGURE 9-7

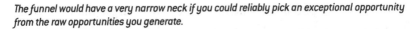

The funnel would have a very narrow neck if you could reliably pick an exceptional opportunity from the raw opportunities you generate.

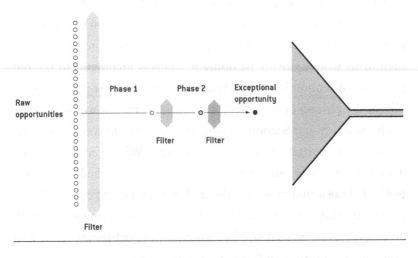

bountiful and beneficial that just building a first prototype without analyzing too many alternatives is often the best way to proceed.[2]

➡ **Cost structure of development tasks.** If innovation tasks are very costly in time or money or both, then you want to do them once and do them right. But if they're cheap, you may prefer to plunge ahead and improvise, knowing that you will refine the opportunity based on what you learn.

➡ **Importance of schedule certainty.** Cascades can be operated according to a strict schedule, whereas the durations of whirlpool-based tournaments are more uncertain. If you must identify an opportunity by a deadline, a cascade may work better.

Much of our discussion and analysis is framed as a cascade, with a steady, straight flow of opportunities from one phase to the next. When you apply these ideas to the reality of your workplace and industry, you will inevitably see some whirling, with opportunities cycling back to previous phases. Often, the earlier exploratory phases work better as cascades, and the intermediate ones of prototyping and testing work better as whirlpools.

For example, figure 9-10 displays the opportunities for a new logo for TerraPass, a retailer of environmental offsets. On the left side are twenty-four proposed logos that designers developed to the point at which the TerraPass team members could evaluate them. Team members concluded that two arrows in what they called the "yin-yang" configuration appealed to the eye and evoked the right brand associations. Based on this learning, the designers developed seven more logos, shown in the middle of the figure. The team then evaluated these in a cascadelike fashion, and one of them ended up being refined to become the final logo. In this case, exploring many opportunities provided insights about the most promising look, themes, and associations for the logo.

FIGURE 9-10

The tournament that resulted in the TerraPass logo included the articulation of about twenty-three alternatives, which led to another seven alternatives of a particular type (the yin-yang arrow theme), one of which was then refined to become the final logo.

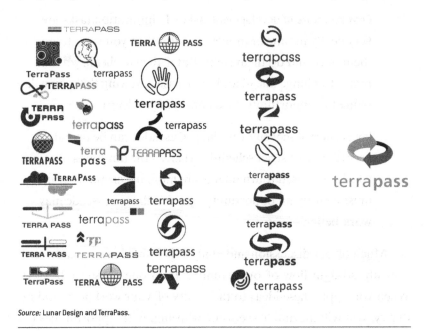

Source: Lunar Design and TerraPass.

SUMMARY

Organizations use tournaments to winnow many opportunities down to the exceptional few that can become profitable innovations. The basic tournament structure used in virtually all organizations is a sequence of development tasks punctuated by selection filters that separate winners and losers. Specific survival rates in the innovation process vary widely across industries and even to some extent within an industry. Filter ratios define the structure of the innovation funnel.

The cost of generating and evaluating opportunities, the variance in their quality, and the importance of the raw opportunity in determining the value of an innovation all help to determine the size of the mouth of your funnel. But as a rule, the quality of the best opportunity increases with the number of opportunities generated and evaluated. Thus, the larger the ratio between the number of opportunities generated and the number commercialized, the higher the quality of the resulting product or service.

Most companies do not generate enough opportunities and could improve the quality of their new products and services by generating more. At the same time, many companies feel pressed to be more innovative and introduce more new opportunities every year. An increase in commercialization without an associated increase in opportunity generation will degrade the quality of your new offerings.

Some innovation tournaments are run as pure cascades, with opportunities flowing in one direction. Others are run as whirlpools, with opportunities flowing back upstream to be transformed and improved. The amount of whirlpooling in an innovation tournament is determined by the potential for learning during the process, the costs of the tournament's phases, and the inflexibility of deadlines.

Diagnostics

→ Do you know the historical flow rates for your innovation pipeline?

→ Did the filter ratios at each phase arise by default or did you choose them deliberately?

→ What would be the cost of doubling the number of raw opportunities you generate and evaluate?

→ How much variation in financial value is exhibited across the innovations in your company or industry?

→ To what extent does the quality of the raw opportunity dictate the value of a launched innovation in your company or industry?

⇒ Are you deliberately choosing the shape of your funnel by considering the cost structure of the phases of innovation and uncertainty you face at each phase?

⇒ Does your funnel operate more like a cascade or more like a whirlpool? Should you shift the mode in one direction or another based on the potential for learning, the cost structure of your development phases, or the importance of schedule certainty?

ADMINISTRATION

Organizing and Governing Innovation

A theme of this book is that innovation can be *managed as a process*. Innovation isn't just hoping for serendipity and counting on bolt-from-the-blue inspirations. Organizational decisions therefore must be made for innovation processes, and yet too often companies fail to make them. As a result, their decisions end up being made informally—if they get made at all.

This chapter focuses on four critical decisions that should shape the organization and governance of your innovation process:

1. How will you configure your organization to generate, sense, and evaluate opportunities?

2. How much will you centralize innovation?

3. Will you foster competition among opportunities in your tournaments?

4. How will you shape your corporate culture of innovation?

CONFIGURING THE ORGANIZATION FOR GENERATING, SENSING, AND EVALUATING OPPORTUNITIES

We have referred to the casting show *American Idol* at other points in this book as an illustration of the tournament approach to innovation. Observe, though, that casting has been around a long time and that the tournament approach to identifying new talent is used throughout the music and entertainment industries. For example, the New York Philharmonic routinely searches for new musicians using auditions. At the time of this writing, it was holding auditions for the positions of principal clarinet, associate principal trombone, and section bass.

An aspiring musician can't just show up at Lincoln Center, ask for an audition, and hope that cheers from the audience will secure her a seat on the stage. Membership in the orchestra is not determined directly by the audience but by Maestro Lorin Maazel, the music director. The Philharmonic's Web site even discourages musicians from submitting recordings of their performances. All the orchestra wants initially is a résumé—chances are, if you have not trained with the right masters and played in the right places, your only way into Lincoln Center will be through the audience door.

If you oppose such an undemocratic approach, you might prefer the means by which YouTube and Newgrounds.com identify talent. At these Web sites, anyone can upload video or audio clips of himself or herself and, in effect, audition before the world. Witness, for example, Gary Brolsma, a chubby guy from Saddle Brook, New Jersey. In 2004, he uploaded to Newgrounds a video entitled "Numa Numa Dance" that showed him lip-synching and wiggling behind his desk to a pop tune. Within three months, several million people had downloaded Brolsma's video, and by 2006, it had been watched an estimated 750 million times.[1] Not even the best violinist in the New York Philharmonic achieves that kind of exposure with such limited resources—or such unorthodox talent.

In the previous chapters, we discussed two key functions of an innovation tournament: *creating* opportunities and *selecting* the exceptional opportunities. The approaches of *American Idol* and the New

York Philharmonic are closely analogous to the options available to companies in identifying and selecting opportunities for innovation.

Companies typically generate about half of their opportunities internally, whether in their research labs or the imaginations of clever salespersons. Opportunities also can be generated externally, including from customers, universities, or independent inventors. The Coca-Cola Company combines the two approaches. It created Diet Coke, Coke Zero, and several other successful beverages internally. But the company also senses opportunities externally, as was the case for several spring water products, as well as the isotonic drink Powerade.

Just as opportunities can be generated internally or externally, they can also be *selected* either internally or externally. As with generation, you'll need to make a decision about what your nexus of selection will be. Previously, we explained Staples's use of tournaments to identify ideas for new products (see chapter 3). Although Staples's customers generate the ideas externally, the company selects from those ideas internally. In contrast, Lutron Electronics, a major producer of lighting controls, allows for external selection, effectively making its customers judges in its innovation tournament. Lutron has thousands of products on the market, many of which are exploratory offerings that, if popular, can become major lines of business. External selection can also be done with customers voting directly on proposed future innovations that are presented online or through mass media.

If you combine the questions of "Where are your opportunities created?" and "Who makes your selection decisions?" you end with four possible organizational configurations, shown in figure 10-1. In the upper right, you see a company such as YouTube that relies on the outside world to create and select opportunities. QVC, the home-shopping retailer, operates in much the same way. It uses innovation contests to find promising products created by small firms and independent inventors. It then offers air time, often at hours when only hardcore shoppers and insomniacs tune in, to gauge initial customer reaction. Why second-guess customers using costly market research when you can just count how many products they order?

FIGURE 10-1

Organizational configurations for the innovation process; level of centralization increases from the upper right to the lower left.

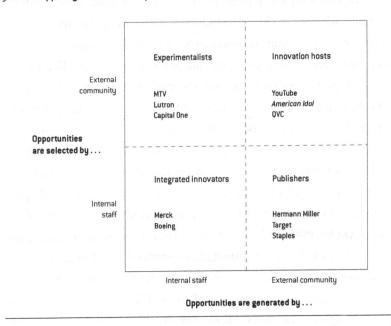

As we move away from the upper right corner of the figure, the level of internal innovation increases. Being internally focused can reduce the variety of a firm's ideas, but it brings the benefits of coordination and efficiency. At the lower left, the innovation process is largely carried out internally.

Four organizational configurations thus emerge:

⇒ Integrated innovators. Innovation happens within the firm, often within a single department. This approach assists in the construction of an efficient portfolio and enables the innovator to target its efforts where they best support its strategic direction. The process can be tightly controlled.

⇒ Experimentalists. These innovators rely on direct market evidence for selection. They generate opportunities internally but test them in public forums and markets to determine which ones deserve further investment.

→ **Publishers.** Publishers excel at selecting rather than creating. They leave opportunity generation to others and count on their insight into consumer behavior to inform their selection decisions. Publishers can exist outside of the media industry. Hermann Miller, the office-furniture seller that introduced the popular Aeron chair, fits in this category. It largely relies on external opportunity creation. Likewise, some large pharmaceutical companies contract with other firms to do early-stage research or monitor biotech start-ups and try to acquire the ones that devise promising therapies.

→ **Innovation hosts.** Innovation hosts such as YouTube and Newgrounds neither need to generate ideas nor make difficult selection decisions. They simply serve as marketplaces where innovation germinates. QVC belongs in this category, too. By selling through cable TV, it has the ability to quickly and cheaply tinker with its array of offerings (external selection based on customer responses). By running innovation contests, the company also obtains new opportunities from independent inventors.

None of these organizational setups is right or wrong. The one that you choose depends on the capabilities of your firm and the environment in which you operate. Maestro Maazel, for example, does not need to rely on audience surveys to determine who excels as a concert violinist. He's an accomplished violinist himself and has directed orchestras around the world. Thanks to his training and experience, he knows what makes a good player and, just as important, understands the skills and sound needed to complement the particular members of the New York Philharmonic. Executives at MTV, in contrast, often don't have such a clear understanding of what constitutes a good opportunity. Consumer tastes in popular media are too fickle and diverse, and what makes for a funny show or a captivating performer in the eyes of the audience is often hard to predict. The only way to find out is to rely on trial and error and external sensing and selection.

Your company's cost structure is also a critical determinant of which approach you take. Boeing cannot simply introduce dozens of airplane designs, which cost of billions of dollars each to develop, and see which one consumers like best.

CENTRALIZING INNOVATION

The second key question is the extent to which you centralize and coordinate your disparate innovation activities. Centralization and co-ordination is largely a moot issue for small companies and new ventures, but becomes prominent for organizations with far-flung operations or broad product lines.

The Opportunity Development Organization

Different organizational forms for innovation usually prevail at different phases in the process, and changes to organizational structure typically occur as opportunities progress. Figure 10-2 shows a structure in which an opportunity development group handles most, if not all, of the opportunities considered by the firm or an operating unit within the firm. (Such groups are sometimes called *business development* or *advanced development*.) At some point, a team will usually be assigned to advance each exceptional opportunity.

Opportunity development groups typically exist at the level of the business unit and also, in multidivisional firms, at the corporate level. At the unit level, the innovation process focuses on new products and services within existing lines of business. At the corporate level, it focuses on discovering and exploiting new lines.[2]

In the early phases of the innovation process, decisions must be made about dozens or even hundreds of opportunities. Having a single development group for the early phases facilitates the comparison of many opportunities and more easily accommodates the high uncertainty about the survival of opportunities. In later phases, ded-

FIGURE 10-2

Exceptional opportunities will usually become projects with team members dedicated to them. An opportunity development group will usually manage opportunities early in the process. Often opportunities are created by champions who come from outside the opportunity development organization.

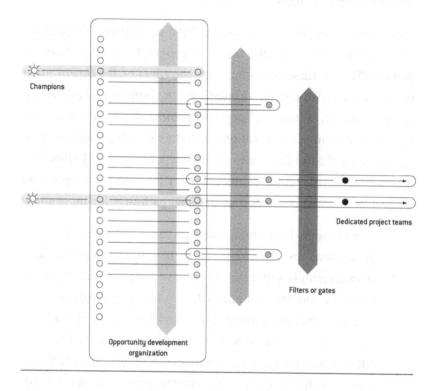

Champions

Dedicated project teams

Filters or gates

Opportunity development organization

icating a team to each opportunity offers advantages of focus, speed, and alignment of incentives.

Even when you employ an opportunity development group, an enthusiastic supporter of an opportunity—a *champion*—may play an important role. The champion need not be a permanent member of the opportunity development organization.

Not all firms use explicitly designated opportunity development groups. Some companies allow opportunities to bubble up from individual innovators or small groups acting on their own. These innovators pursue their ideas using slack time provided for that purpose. Once an opportunity begins to require significant resources, the firm formally evaluates it and makes it part of the firmwide portfolio of opportunities.

Coordinating the Edges and the Core

Large companies tend to be formed from collections of operating units, which may be divided based on geography, product lines, or markets. We call these operating units the *edges* of the organization because they are located at the interface—the front line—between the company and its customers. Large companies will almost always also include some centralized functions, including possibly a central innovation group. We call these centralized functions the *core*. Figure 10-3 portrays an organization composed of a core and five operating units. The figure also shows four possible pathways for innovation.

- **Core to edges.** In the first pathway, the central innovation group develops opportunities and then rolls them out to the operating units. Often, the edges have a say in which opportunities the company commercializes—they participate in filtering. Overall, however, innovation happens like broadcasting: a central transmitter sends out the message. The McDonald's restaurant chain takes this approach: experimentation happens centrally, and new products flow outward to the restaurants.

- **Edge.** A second pathway happens at an edge with little or no core involvement. Bowing to the diversity of tastes around the world, many multinational food companies, for example, have country subsidiaries with their own research and development groups. The core plays little or no role in their innovation decisions. Many companies in other industries are similarly dispersed geographically, especially if they have grown by acquisition.

- **Edge to edge.** A third pathway allows innovations pioneered at one edge to be transferred to another. The transfer might

FIGURE 10-3

Four pathways for innovation involving a centralized innovation organization and operating units.

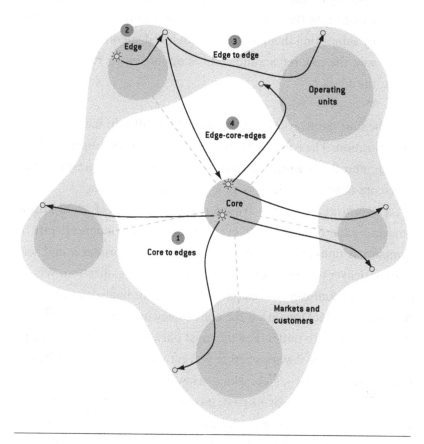

occur thanks to informal relationships among staff members, or the core might broker it. Organizational mechanisms such as companywide conferences or rotation programs can facilitate this exchange.

➡ **Edge-core-edge.** A fourth pathway starts at the edge, goes to the core, and then radiates back out to one or more edges. Consider the work that is done by professional services organization such as Deloitte. In general, innovation in professional services happens as teams at the edges devise

new solutions for their clients' problems. But such decentralization risks multiple teams wasting time and money by
working on the same sorts of problems. To prevent that,
teams make their innovations available to the rest of the firm
by submitting them to the core. In an edge-core-edge pathway, the core refines and codifies opportunities recognized at
the edges.

The four pathways shown in figure 10-3 differ in their degree of
centralization. The core-to-edge approach is the most centralized approach, and the edge-only approach is the most decentralized. The
edge-core-edge and edge-to-edge approaches are hybrids.

The centralized approach confers the advantages of standardization and scale economies. If every edge operates independently, a
company is unlikely to be able to standardize its products and services or deliver them efficiently across the entire organization. What's
more, it risks confusing its customers with uncoordinated experiments.
A strength of McDonald's is the consistency in its quality and offerings from outlet to outlet. For the most part, you see the same menu
and taste the same flavors whether you eat your Big Mac in Philadelphia or San Francisco, Nebraska or Hawaii.[3]

Decentralization, for its part, has advantages, too. It enables innovation to happen close to the customers, so the innovators have
deep market knowledge and can quickly test-drive new ideas. It allows for a dramatic increase in innovative capacity because most
companies have more people working at the edges than at the core. It
also permits more experimentation. Not only are more people working on innovation, but also their experiments do not have to be approved and vetted by a central clearinghouse.

You can combine the approaches and thus benefit from the
strengths of each. The trick lies in emphasizing the approaches at different times in the life cycle of a business. When a company operates
in an emerging market in which dynamic response to changing conditions is important, it should favor a decentralized approach. At a
time like this, proximity to the customer and quick experimentation

outweigh any inefficiencies created by duplication and lack of coordination. Set growth targets, and let the edges make their own decisions about how to meet them. When a firm is operating in a mature market and worrying over costs, however, centralization works better. It improves efficiency, thanks to practices like centralized sourcing and product-line rationalization. As Joel Spira, founder of Lutron Electronics, puts it, "Chaos increases new business. Order increases profits."[4]

COMPETITION AMONG OPPORTUNITIES AND RELATIVE COMPARISON

The very idea of a tournament conjures up images of contestants vying for advantage. But most tournaments include a mix of *absolute* quality hurdles, which opportunities must clear, and *relative* comparisons in which the best opportunities in a group are selected for further development. For *American Idol*, the staff initially screens a huge number of contestants against the absolute criterion of reasonable singing ability. Only later, after hundreds of thousands of candidates have been winnowed to fewer than one hundred, do the relative comparisons occur. Most tournaments involve both relative and absolute evaluations. Each approach has pros and cons.

Relative comparison lets you factor construction of your innovation portfolio into your selection process (see chapter 7). You can match the number of opportunities selected with the capacity of your pipeline. Relative comparison also introduces competition among opportunities, which forces advocates to burnish their opportunities and clearly articulate the advantages. With absolute hurdles, in contrast, firms never face the discipline of a fixed quota and so can drift toward lax quality standards, flooding their pipelines with marginal opportunities. Conversely, the organization could become so picky that no opportunities are ever deemed good enough.

Of course, relative comparison can sometimes lead to the advancement of weak opportunities, too. Maybe you've hit a dry spell in your opportunity creation. If so, relative comparison can lull you into believing that the opportunities that you've selected promise exceptional value. After all, they won in your carefully constructed and rigorously implemented competition. But in reality, the tournament attracted a weak field. Conversely, in a strong field, opportunities may be eliminated that, under more normal conditions, would stand out. Relative comparison can also be unwieldy. Simply put, it's tough to compare lots of opportunities. Relative comparisons make sense only when considering fewer than fifty opportunities.

A final disadvantage of a relative comparison is that it can bog down the innovation process. Relative comparison requires that you assemble a set of opportunities into a batch and consider them side by side. You may fail to advance an amazing opportunity quickly enough because you're waiting until it can be compared with a hundred others or discussed at your quarterly review meeting. A solution is to fast-track any opportunity that clears a high-quality hurdle and fill the rest of your pipeline with the best opportunities from big batches.

CREATING A CULTURE OF INNOVATION

The idea of shaping culture implies that you as a manager know what culture you want. If you do, good for you. Having that clear sense and regularly communicating it to your staff is the first step to shaping your organization's culture. Innovation leaders like W. L. Gore & Associates make their culture of innovation explicit. Gore uses a diagram similar to that in figure 10-4 to articulate its culture and values. Many of the elements of this overall culture are critical to the way it pursues innovation. You, too, can take actions to guide and reinforce the culture of innovation in your organization. We suggest five here.

Incentives and Recognition

If you care about your culture of innovation, your first focus should be recognition and rewards. The most powerful rewards are career

FIGURE 10-4

An example of the articulation of culture by an organization. W. L. Gore's diagram of its culture comprises (a) the core, (b) its values, and (c) its practices. Gore's diagram reflects its entire culture, of which many elements relate to the way it innovates. ASOP refers to Associates' Stock Ownership Plan. Waterline refers to respect for the level of financial risk undertaken (i.e., are we drilling a hole in the boat below the waterline?).

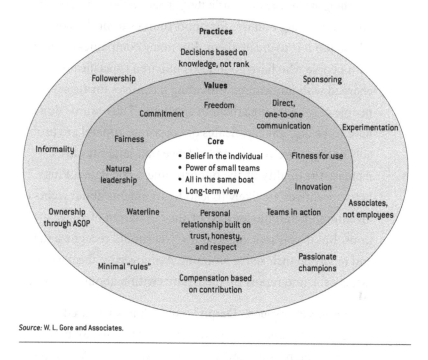

Source: W. L. Gore and Associates.

advancement and greater responsibility. How you make decisions about those matters will signal strongly the values of your organization. Several innovation measures are obviously important here, such as the quality and quantity of opportunities identified, the tenacity of individuals and teams in solving problems, and the care and quality of execution of screening and analyzing opportunities. However, three more subtle behaviors may be worth rewarding, too.

⇒ **Celebrating failure.** Halting an unpromising investment is one of the most important actions a person can take. It allows resources to be applied elsewhere. Doing it early can save millions. Yet people tend not to celebrate the termination of bad investments in the way that they do the selection of good ones. Making a mantra out of the slogan "Fail early, fail often, and fail inexpensively" will remind your employees that every good innovation tournament entails failure.

➡ **Providing incentives for contributing opportunities.** We do not advocate paying bonuses for opportunities to professionals whose job it is to create them. But many companies are filled with people who have good ideas but aren't specifically charged with innovating. Providing incentives for these people may encourage them to speak up. The rewards don't have to be big; gift certificates or corporate apparel are probably enough. We've seen no evidence that larger rewards increase the quality of the opportunities articulated. Plus, hefty incentives are likely to lead to arguments about rights of inventorship and the fairness of the evaluation of suggestions. But if you seek suggestions, you should recognize them and report on their status promptly. Acknowledge them within, say, a week and report on their status within about a month.

➡ **Recognizing champions.** Despite our faith in structured processes for managing innovation tournaments, we believe that personal passion and advocacy have crucial roles in the development of exceptional opportunities. Even advocacy that challenges the judgment of the majority is valuable. It forces a careful evaluation of what may be an opportunity with tremendous, but unrecognized, potential. Praise, in an e-mail message or as a comment during a performance review, shows the value your organization places on its opportunity champions.

Transparency and Rules for Tournaments

Most opportunities will not result in commercially successful innovation, and transparency in your processes and decision making soothes the egos of people whose projects get killed. Besides, if your process is logical and fair, letting your staff see and understand that will only enhance their faith in what you're doing. This is one of the strengths of the tournament approach to innovation: as long as the rules are clear, everyone will understand that a tournament has more losers than winners.

To help ensure transparency, you should require people to describe each opportunity in the same format, using a template. Templates can be used for articulating opportunities, analyzing financial value, describing solution concepts, and completing performance reviews, among other tasks. They can be as simple as a set of questions posed on a form or a standard format for presentation of graphics.

Physical Arrangement of the Workplace

Research dating to the 1960s has proved that the physical arrangement of people has a huge influence on their communication.[5] Changing an office environment can shape a corporate culture. An action as simple as placing a nice cappuccino machine in a common area can stimulate informal interactions. Mixing staff from different functional areas—for example, marketing and engineering—can also foster better collaboration. Open-plan workspaces likewise improve the flow of information. In both cases, ideas may spring up as previously separated parts of the staff start to interact. And recall that, in an innovation tournament, opportunities that are wacky and of highly variable quality improve the overall performance of the innovation system.

The physical arrangement of your workplace also sends signals to your prospective employees. If you want people who enjoy collaboration, an open floor plan that fosters informal chats will be more likely to attract them than a warren of private offices.

Recruiting Process

Your people are your culture. How you recruit new employees communicates powerfully not only with the newcomers but also with those already on staff. Take Google's tactic of placing difficult technical problems in publications and challenging potential employees to submit solutions. That attracts self-confident, smart applicants and also reinforces a culture of meritocracy and rationality. What does your recruiting reveal about your culture? Is your process consistent with the elements of culture you wish to reinforce?

Slack Time

Several firms, among them Google, 3M, and Genentech, use the idea of "20 percent time"—a scheme by which employees can spend up to 20 percent of their work time pursuing any innovation opportunity that piques their curiosity. We admit that this may not be an optimal way to allocate staff hours—some employees probably should invest much more than 20 percent, and some much less. But it is administratively straightforward, and it communicates the values of trust and individual initiative. Once the opportunity has grown beyond its infancy, it can enter a more formal innovation tournament.

SUMMARY

There are multiple ways to organize your company for innovation. You can leave the creation of opportunities to others and focus on selection. You can be an experimentalist, generating opportunities but leaving the selection of the winning ones to the market. Or you can simply act as a host of the innovation process and let creative folks from outside your organization pitch their ideas to your customers.

Besides choosing an organizational structure, you need to decide how centralized your innovation process will be. Centralization brings efficiency but also suffers from the Soviet syndrome: planning and coordination often squelch creativity. Decentralization, in contrast, enables quick experimentation and creates many opportunities but also breeds inefficiency. Often, a hybrid setup makes sense.

You can evaluate opportunities in isolation, comparing them with an absolute quality hurdle, or you can let them compete against each other. Both approaches are likely to be used in your tournaments.

Finally, you can shape the innovation culture of your organization by fine-tuning incentives, making innovation tournaments transparent, creating an attractive and open workplace, and recruiting staff in ways that underscore your values.

Diagnostics

→ Have you considered alternative configurations of your organization, perhaps relying on external entities for a greater fraction of the innovation activities in which you engage?

→ How do you structure the evaluation of many innovation opportunities? Do you have an organizational unit that considers all early opportunities simultaneously? At what point in the process are dedicated teams deployed?

→ How do you sense the most promising innovation occurring at the periphery of the organization? How do you deploy the best opportunities across a distributed firm?

→ What is the role of the core in your innovation process and what is the role of the edges? Is your innovation process centralized or decentralized?

→ Who decides how resources are allocated to opportunities and what opportunities are moved forward? Is the process transparent?

→ What culture do you aspire to? Have you articulated it? What levers have you acted on to achieve that culture?

TOURNAMENTS 201

An Innovator's Guide

to Getting Started

Chances are that all readers of this book have at least one thing in common—they want their organizations to be more innovative. The mere desire to be more innovative, however, is hard to turn into action. Organizations tend to follow a similar pattern, improving performance by progressing along a common path. In this chapter, we introduce an *innovation maturity model* consisting of five levels, a path toward achieving innovation excellence.[1] After defining the path, we outline next steps for both organizations just starting out and those that are more mature in their development.

THE INNOVATION MATURITY MODEL

Defining a common improvement path in the form of a maturity model is helpful for at least two reasons. First, it creates a shared vision of excellence and hence gives a clear direction for an organization to improve its innovation process. Second, it acknowledges that organizations differ in how far along they are in their innovation journey. The right next steps for an organization at the beginning of the journey differ from those for a company farther along. We divide the path to innovation excellence into five levels.

Level 1: Reactive

At level 1, innovation typically happens in response to external forces. A customer wants an improved version of a product, a competitor swipes market share, or a regulation forces new ways of doing business. A few people in the organization step up and spearhead the effort. Often, these ad hoc innovators have to sidestep existing rules and procedures and hunt for needed resources. They develop opportunities while keeping their efforts hidden from top management until the new product or service has matured enough to be presented almost as a fait accompli. If senior managers track innovation at all, they do so through aggregate measures such as spending rates, and through marketing metrics like market share and sales growth. As a result, they tend to measure innovation only retrospectively.

Level 2: Structured

In level 2 organizations, top executives have declared innovation a corporate goal. Often, they've designated someone as the chief innovation officer, and they pepper the company's annual report with the word *innovation*. The firm begins to use structured innovation processes, possibly even companywide innovation tournaments. (Don't confuse innovation processes with the widely used phase-gate process that many firms apply to product development. Innovation processes include the identification of a portfolio of exceptional opportunities, whereas most phase-gate processes take the opportunity as a given and focus on pushing a particular project through the development stages.) Managers might employ formal measures of innovativeness such as the percentage of revenue obtained from recently launched products and services. Measurement continues to focus on past innovations rather than looking forward to what's in the pipeline.

Level 3: In Control

A level 3 organization moves from simply having an innovation process to designing one that fits its strategic needs. Managers effectively monitor the process using measures such as the number of opportunities at each phase, the cost of identifying opportunities, filter ratios, and financial outcomes. Based on this information, they tune process design, pondering the make-or-buy decision ("What types of opportunities should we pursue internally?"), the magnitude of filter ratios ("What's the optimal shape of our funnel?"), and the allocation of innovative capacity ("Where should the bottleneck be in our innovation process?").

Level 3 managers also use portfolio tools to guide the creation of new opportunities and adjust selection criteria to favor opportunities with high strategic value. This allows the organization to move more nimbly and prepare for a variety of future scenarios, possibly by experimenting with a few horizon 3 opportunities. Performance measurement becomes more sophisticated. It links firm-level growth with innovation activities using the portfolio tools outlined in chapter 7. Measures are thus not only backward looking, but also look at expected future financial performance based on the current state of the innovation pipeline.

Level 4: Internalized

The transition to level 4 is largely organizational. Whereas the driving force behind innovation at levels 2 and 3 is usually senior management, level 4 organizations have fully internalized the importance of innovation. The innovation processes are fully embraced throughout the organization without senior management pushing for them. The process discipline and the portfolio planning tools of a level 3 organization enable the organization to benefit from the tension between top-down and bottom-up forces. Without mastery of the structure of level 3, empowering everyone to innovate can lead an organization into chaos and frustration.

Executives continue to focus on setting strategic direction through portfolio planning, and the innovation portfolio is robust (see chapter 7). The organization is thus prepared for changes in its operating environment as they arise. Although the firm's strategic intent is clear, individual employees still have sufficient time, knowledge, freedom, and resources to conceive of opportunities in any domain and to submit them to innovation tournaments.

Level 5: Continuously Improving

Even the best process benefits from continuous improvement. Just as quality circles or kaizen teams improve manufacturing systems, so too innovation processes can be improved continuously. Staff members in level 5 organizations have mastered all of the tools and approaches of levels 1 through 4. They continuously measure the performance of their innovation process and seek ways to fine-tune it. For example, they monitor the accuracy of old forecasts and use that information to tweak current forecasts. They fully integrate innovation management with financial planning. Table 11-1 summarizes the five levels.

FIRST STEP FOR A DEVELOPING ORGANIZATION: THE INNOVATION WORKSHOP

Ultimately, there's only one way to learn to swim—you have to get wet. No amount of poolside calisthenics or video study can substitute for plunging in. The same holds for the first step along the path

TABLE 11-1

Five levels of the innovation maturity model. Most companies progress along a similar pathway from level 1 to level 5.

	Level 1: Reactive	Level 2: Structured	Level 3: In control	Level 4: Internalized	Level 5: Continuously improving
People	Individual heroic action; artisan skills	Senior management makes innovation a priority	Senior management defines innovation strategy and use of portfolio planning tools and/or defines selection criteria that favor projects that implement strategy	Companywide use of innovation tools; creation of opportunities is directed toward the strategic objective (as opposed to just the selection); slack time for employees to allow for bottom-up innovation	Continuous dialogue between top-down and bottom-up
Process	No formal process exists	Senior management makes innovation a priority	Innovation activities follow the overall process	Process is consciously designed; decisions about filter ratios, make–buy, buffers, etc., are made	Ongoing optimization
Performance measures	Growth	New product ratios	Flow measures for all the phases, including output (return curve)	Detailed measurement of forecasts (financials, POS)	Ongoing measurement and feedback to decision makers
Purpose	Response to external shocks (client needs, legislation, technical challenges); defensive: focus largely on horizons 1 and 2	Formalize and structure innovation activities; increase overall innovativeness; focus is on growth	Identify specific opportunities and threats to quickly react to change and to prepare for scenarios and/or experiment with horizon 3 opportunities	Build a robust portfolio attractive across a range of possible future states of the world	Actively seek change and disruption

to innovation excellence. Eventually, instead of discussing theories, paying consultants, or reading more books, you have to get started.

An important concept in the literature on change management is the "small win."[2] To get people excited, to create buzz, and to build momentum, you have to accomplish something meaningful without too big of an initial resource commitment. We've found that a one-day innovation workshop can often deliver just the sort of win that you need.

An innovation workshop typically engages twenty to forty employees. For small organizations, this might account for a big chunk of the staff. For bigger ones, you might organize multiple workshops. Either way, recruit as diverse a group of participants as possible. Mix employees across various departments—don't hold one workshop for marketers and another for accountants.

Table 11-2 provides a possible schedule for a one-day workshop. It should start with opening remarks from a senior executive stressing the firm's commitment to innovation, innovation's role in the company's future, and some past internal innovation successes. The mod-

TABLE 11-2

Outline of a one-day innovation workshop with associated preparation tasks. This suggested workshop emphasizes the creation and screening of opportunities. A workshop like this will typically result in over one hundred opportunities, of which twenty to forty will be presented, and a handful are likely to emerge as exceptional.

	Time line for innovation workshop	Preparation for workshop
8:00	Motivation and opening comments.	Invite 20–40 people. Create groups of 4–6 people each.
8:15	Overview of process and mini-lecture on innovation tournaments. (See slide deck.)	Select voting method.
9:30	Opportunity identification (individual and group).	Prepare emergency stimuli sheet.
10:30	Pitch opportunities. Multi-vote (either stickers or electronic).	Have a bell ready to enforce 2-minute rule.
12:00	Lunch break	Download slide decks from InnovationTournaments.com.
1:00	Classify opportunities into horizons 1–3. Identify most promising opportunities. Discuss strategic needs.	Flip charts or transparencies for describing opportunities.
2:00	Identify roadblocks to pursuing most promising opportunities.	
3:00	Articulate action items.	

erator then provides an overview of the tournament framework outlined in this book.

In the next phase, about an hour into the workshop, the participants focus on identifying opportunities. You might allow participants to work on any product or service challenge, or ask them to address a specific strategic need. We find that groups are most productive if individuals spend about twenty minutes working alone. Each of them will probably identify five or more opportunities. For workshop participants who are struggling to generate ideas for opportunities, you can hand out a one-page "emergency stimulus package" to help spark their creativity. (See "Emergency Stimuli" for an example of such a sheet for a company seeking opportunities related to health and wellness.)

After the individual phase, assemble groups of four or five participants and ask them to discuss the opportunities that each of the group's members conceived. Instruct them to also identify any additional opportunities that may arise in discussion. Each group will then pick its best opportunities, usually one for every member of the group, to be pitched to the larger group of twenty to forty people. You'll thus usually end up with about as many opportunities as you have participants. We suggest that you also allow individuals to pitch opportunities that they feel passionate about but that, for whatever reason, their small group didn't pick. All presentations should adhere to the 2-1-0 rule: a two-minute presentation and one slide or poster per opportunity, with no questions or discussion. Once all the pitches have been made, the group votes on the most promising opportunities, using one of the methods in chapter 4 (e.g., stickers applied to flip-chart sheets).

The participants then can discuss the next steps needed to advance the most promising opportunities. The discussion might touch on how to classify opportunities according to the three horizons, how to increase the efficacy of the firm's opportunity generation, or how to remove organizational and personal roadblocks that prevent employees from being more innovative in their daily work.

Emergency Stimuli

➡ What do you expect to be the major societal trends in the next ten years? What new needs for health and wellness will be created by these trends?

➡ What unique products and services are being offered in peripheral geographic or regulatory markets? Might some of these services be offered in the mainstream markets?

➡ Which products and services are highly fragmented and might benefit substantially from being rolled into an integrated firm?

➡ What premium product or service might be taken downmarket and delivered directly to consumers, say through a Wal-Mart or other mass distribution channel?

➡ What is a source of personal frustration for you with respect to health and wellness? How might this frustration be better addressed?

A large organization might opt to collect the opportunities conceived in several internal workshops and combine them in a single companywide tournament. One way to combine and evaluate a large number of opportunities across a geographically distributed organization is with the Darwinator software (available at www.Innovation Tournaments.com).

A key advantage of the workshop is that it is a specific task that you can implement without a large commitment of resources. The workshop also helps participants to appreciate the power of innovation tournaments. It creates an experience and a language that your organization can then use to tackle the organizational challenge of moving to a higher level of innovation maturity. Once you've completed a workshop, you can begin to address many of the other issues identified in this book.

NEXT STEPS FOR A MATURING ORGANIZATION

Once you have run your first innovation tournament and there is a basic tournament structure in place for the creation and selection of opportunities, chances are that you'll find yourself asking "Is this the best way for us to run these innovation tournaments?" To make the transition from level 2 to level 3, we suggest that you collect and analyze data about your current innovation process. Here are some steps for performing this analysis:

⇒ Define the phases of the innovation tournaments used in your organization and count how many opportunities exited each phase over a given time period, say a year.

⇒ Determine the number of opportunities currently in process at each phase in your innovation tournament or tournaments. Based on this information, compute your filter ratios and the probability of success of an opportunity at each phase.

⇒ Investigate the origins of your opportunities. What are your sources of the opportunities? How much does it cost you to create an additional opportunity?

With this information, you can then tackle the question of whether you would benefit from widening the mouth of the funnel. As we asserted in previous chapters, *most organizations don't create enough opportunities*. If they need to launch five products a year and have determined that 10 percent of their opportunities tend to reach the market, then they create fifty opportunities. But, as we have argued in chapter 9, you can do much better than that. If it is not a lot more expensive to generate one hundred opportunities, you are likely to be much better off identifying one hundred and then picking the best fifty.

Armed with your data, you can revisit most of the diagnostic questions at the end of the preceding chapters. This time be ready to provide responses to even the more quantitative questions. Additional resources for improving performance can be found in the appendix.

MORE TOOLS AND OUR WEB SITE

To help you focus on your innovation journey and to apply the principles of innovation tournaments within your organization, we have compiled a library of supporting materials, available online at www.InnovationTournaments.com, including the following:

- PowerPoint slides of the figures in this book and sample presentations that you can use for your innovation workshops

- Excel spreadsheets to quickly create innovation return curves and Real-Win-Worth-it evaluations

- The Darwinator software, which lets you run tournaments with a group of participants over the Web

- An annotated bibliography of many of the most important books and articles on innovation management

➡ Readings and case studies on topics such as open innovation, outsourcing, performance measurement, and research on opportunity identification and creativity

All this material is ready for download and free of charge, enabling you to quickly obtain some small wins as you run your first innovation tournaments—small wins that we hope will lead to big results.

Introduction

1. Assumes life cycle revenues and profit margins typical for the industry. See Aaron Smith, "Merck's Other Big Problem: Zocor," CNNMoney.com, January 30, 2006, http://money.cnn.com/2006/01/30/news/companies/merck/index.htm.

2. See Dan Moren, "Analysis: Inside Apple's iPod Sales Figures," Macworld.com, January 31, 2008, http://www.macworld.com/article/131874/2008/01/ipodsales.html for sales data; R&D data and spending levels of Apple's competitors are based on the authors' research.

3. "Ritz Roulette £1.3m Win Scam," GamblingGates.com, December 7, 2004, http://www.gamblinggates.com/news/casino/ritz_roulette_scam24041.html.

4. The iPod also relied on the iTunes desktop music management software, itself an existing technology developed previously by a small company.

5. This graph was inspired by a study by the Boston Consulting Group, *Innovation 2006* (Boston: The Boston Consulting Group, 2006), http://www.bcg.com/impact_expertise/publications/files/2006_Innovation_Survey_report.pdf.

6. We conducted the same analysis for chemicals, pharmaceuticals, and autos. No consistent relationship is evident between R&D spending and performance.

7. Terwiesch and colleagues provide one of the few empirical studies relating firm-level R&D spending to financial performance. See Christian Terwiesch, Christoph H. Loch, and Martin Niederkofler, "When Product Development Performance Makes a Difference: A Statistical Analysis in the Electronics Industry," *Journal of Product Innovation Management* 15, no. 1 (1998): 3–15.

8. All values shown are adjusted for the probability of success of the innovation. So, for example, a 50 percent chance of profits of $80 million would be shown as an expected value of $40 million. Furthermore, all figures are *present*

values, accounting for the opportunity cost of the capital and the timing of the cash flows.

9. See, for example, G. C. O'Connor, R. Leifer, A. S. Paulson, and L. S. Peters, *Grabbing Lightning: Building a Capability for Breakthrough Innovation* (San Francisco: Jossey-Bass, 2008).

Chapter 1

1. Data about *American Idol* are taken from http://en.wikipedia.org/wiki/American_idol, accessed August 11, 2008.

2. E. Von Weizsacker, A. B. Lovins, and L. H. Lovins, *Factor of Four: Doubling Wealth and Halving Resource Use* (London: Earthscan, 1997).

3. The theory underlying open innovation tournaments is explained in C. Terwiesch and Y. Xu, "Innovation Contests," *Management Science* 54, no. 9 (2008): 1529–1543. Published online before print July 25, 2008, http://mansci.journal.informs.org/cgi/content/abstract/54/9/1529. There are various ways to categorize the sources of innovation. See, for example, P. Drucker, "The Discipline of Innovation," *Harvard Business Review*, November–December 1998, 149–157.

4. X Prize Foundation, "The X Prize Heritage," http://www.xprize.org/about/the-x-prize-heritage.

5. Sommer and Loch have researched this issue extensively. See S. C. Sommer and C. H. Loch, "Selectionism and Learning in Projects with Complexity and Unforeseeable Uncertainty," *Management Science* 50, no. 10 (2004): 1334–1347. See also Lee Fleming and Olav Sorensen, "Science as a Map in Technological Search," *Strategic Management Journal* 25 (2004): 909–928.

6. This figure is inspired by the research of Dahan and Mendelson, who apply the statistical tools of extreme value theory to the area of innovation. For more details, see E. Dahan and H. Mendelson, "An Extreme Value Model of Concept Testing," *Management Science* 47, no. 1 (2001): 102–116.

Chapter 2

1. Figure 1-11 in the previous chapter analyzes this more formally. Also see P. Drucker, "The Discipline of Innovation," *Harvard Business Review*, November–December 1998, 149–157, and R. Leifer, C. M. McDermott, G. C. O'Connor, and L. S. Peters, *Radical Innovation: How Mature Companies Can Outsmart Upstarts* (Boston: Harvard Business School Press, 2000).

2. B. Nalebuff and I. Ayres, *Why Not? How to Use Everyday Ingenuity to Solve Problems Big and Small* (Boston: Harvard Business School Press, 2003);

Scott A. Shane, *Finding Fertile Ground: Identifying Extraordinary Opportunities for New Ventures* (Upper Saddle River, NJ: Wharton School Publishing, 2005).

3. Alan Lafley, "Why P&G's Smile Is So Bright," *Business Week*, August 12, 2002, 58.

4. W. Chan Kim and Renée Mauborgne, *Blue Ocean Strategy* (Boston: Harvard Business School Press, 2005).

5. Ibid.

6. Note that from a methodological perspective, the dots in figure 2-4 should not be connected because there exists no logic to the ordering of the attributes and the value of the y-axis really has no meaning at the midpoint between two attributes. Yet, given that this form of attribute map is widely used in practice, we use this format in figure 2-4.

7. K. Girotra, C. Terwiesch, and K. Ulrich, "Idea Generation and the Quality of the Best Idea," working paper, The Wharton School, Philadelphia, 2007.

8. There exists some research that links idea generation to personality as measured by the commonly used Myers-Briggs survey. See G. A. Stevens and J. Burley, "Piloting the Rocket of Radical Innovation," *Research Technology Management* 46, no. 2 (2000): 16–26.

9. J. Goldenberg and D. Mazursky, *Creativity in Product Innovation* (Cambridge, UK: Cambridge University Press, 2002).

10. For the substantial body of research that has been done on this topic, see M. Diehl and W. Stroebe, "Productivity Loss in Brainstorming Groups: Towards the Solution of a Riddle," *Journal of Personality and Social Psychology* 52, no. 3 (1987): 497–509.

Chapter 3

1. Wikipedia, "Red Bull," July 2007, http://en.wikipedia.org/wiki/Red_bull.

2. John Dodge, "Will Boeing's 787 Dreamliner Improve the Flying Experience?" *Design News,* June 4, 2007, 11.

3. Wikipedia, "Nintendo Wii," March 2008, http://en.wikipedia.org/wiki/Nintendo_Wii.

4. E. Von Hippel, *The Sources of Innovation* (Oxford: Oxford University Press, 1988).

5. T. Åstebro, "The Return to Independent Invention: Evidence of Unrealistic Optimism, Risk Seeking, or Skewness Loving?" *The Economic Journal* 113 (2003): 226–239.

6. A wide range of business models exist that support innovation tournaments directly or indirectly. See H. Chesbrough, *Open Business Models: How to*

Thrive in the New Innovation Landscape (Boston: Harvard Business School Press, 2006).

7. Scott A. Shane, *Academic Entrepreneurship: University Spinoffs and Wealth Creation* (Cheltenham, UK: Edward Elgar Publishing, 2004).

8. Andrew Kramer, "These Boots Were Made for 22 M.P.H.," *The New York Times*, March 17, 2007.

9. L. Fleming and M. Marx, "Managing Creativity in Small Worlds," *California Management Review* 48, no. 4 (2006): 6–27.

Chapter 4

1. Reuters, July 24, 2006.

2. VanGundy discusses the question of how many votes each participant should be endowed with. See Arthur B. VanGundy, *Techniques of Structured Problem Solving*, 2nd ed. (New York: Van Nostrand Reinhold, 1988).

3. For example, the company TurningPoint offers little remote controls (about as large as a small pocket calculator) that allow participants to submit votes to a computer.

4. VanGundy uses the term *hot-spots* and discusses how to handle them. See VanGundy, *Techniques of Structured Problem Solving.*

5. The data are taken from K. Girotra, C. Terwiesch, and K. T. Ulrich, "Drug Development at Merck Research Labs," case study (Philadelphia: The Wharton School, 2004).

6. We are grateful to George Day for sharing these criteria with us. These criteria were also used as the basis for table 4-3. See George S. Day and Paul J. H. Schoemaker, *Peripheral Vision: Detecting the Weak Signals That Will Make or Break Your Company* (Boston: Harvard Business School Press, 2006).

7. Also see R. Leifer, C. M. McDermott, G. C. O'Connor, and L. S. Peters, *Radical Innovation: How Mature Companies Can Outsmart Upstarts* (Boston: Harvard Business School Press, 2000).

8. Day and Schoemaker, in *Peripheral Vision*, have mapped numerical values for the probability of success onto this map.

9. Mehrdad Baghai, Stephen Coley, and David White, *The Alchemy of Growth* (Reading, MA: Perseus Books Group, 2000); Tim Koller, Marc Goedhart, and David Wessels, *Valuation: Measuring and Managing the Value of Companies*, 4th ed. (Hoboken, NJ: John Wiley and Sons, 2005).

10. The strategic bucket method has been described in a number of articles, yet the work by Chao and Kavadias is the first to provide a rigorous justification

for this method. See R. O. Chao and S. Kavadias, "A Theoretical Framework for Managing the New Product Development Portfolio: When and How to Use Strategic Buckets," *Management Science* 54, no. 5 (2008): 907–921.

Chapter 5

1. See Constantinos C. Markides and Paul A. Geroski, *Fast Second: How Smart Companies Bypass Radical Innovation to Enter and Dominate New Markets* (San Francisco: Jossey-Bass, 2005) for a very elegant way of articulating a business strategy based on a set of simple questions. Loch and DeMeyer provide an excellent application to the R&D setting. See A. DeMeyer and C. Loch, "Technology Strategy," in *Handbook of New Product Development Management*, eds. C. Loch and S. Kavadias (Hoboken, NJ: John Wiley and Sons, 1996). Loch and Tapper also use the Markides framework and show how one can translate the business strategy to an R&D strategy. See Christoph H. Loch and U. A. Staffan Tapper, "Implementing a Strategy-Driven Performance Measurement System for an Applied Research Group," *Journal of Product Innovation Management* 19, no. 3 (2003): 185–198.

2. The term *blue ocean strategy* was coined by Kim and Maurgogne to reflect an uncontested market space. See W. C. Kim and R. Mauborgne, *Blue Ocean Strategy: How to Create Uncontested Market Space and Make Competition Irrelevant* (Boston: Harvard Business School Press, 2005).

3. K. T. Ulrich and S. D. Eppinger, "Identifying Customer Needs," in *Product Design and Development*, 4th ed. (New York: McGraw-Hill/Irwin, 2008).

4. J. B. Barney, "Firm Resources and Sustained Competitive Advantage," *Journal of Management* 17, no. 1 (1991): 99–120.

5. See C. Perez, *Technological Revolutions and Financial Capital: The Dynamics of Bubbles and Golden Ages* (Northhampton, MA: Edward Elgar Publishing, 2003) for a more detailed discussion on life cycles. Also see DeMeyer and Loch, "Technology Strategy," for an excellent discussion of this topic. The initial research in this area goes back to W. J. Abernathy and J. M. Utterback, "Patterns of Industrial Innovation," *Technology Review,* June–July 1978, 41–47.

6. G. A. Moore, *Dealing with Darwin: How Great Companies Innovate at Every Phase of Their Evolution.* (New York: Portfolio, 2005) discusses how several industries evolve.

7. James Utterback, *Mastering the Dynamics of Innovation* (Boston: Harvard Business School Press, 1994).

8. Daniel Snow, "Extraordinary Efficiency Growth in Response to New Technology Entries: The Carburetor's 'Last Gasp,'" Academy of Management Conference Series, 2004.

9. For more discussions on innovation strategy, see Rita G. McGrath and Ian MacMillan, *The Entrepreneurial Mindset* (Boston: Harvard Business School Press, 2000); also see G. Hamel and C. K. Prahalad, *Competing for the Future* (Boston: Harvard Business School Press, 1996).

Chapter 6

1. Loch and colleagues provide an excellent discussion of project risk management, especially with respect to dealing with unknown unknowns. See C. H. Loch, A. DeMeyer, and M. T. Pich, *Managing the Unknown: A New Approach to Managing High Uncertainty and Risk in Projects* (New York: John Wiley and Sons, 2006).

2. In general, you can't just divide the expected values of two random variables and get the expected value of the quotient. However, in this case, we assume that the investment quantity was known with certainty, and thus we're dividing the expected profits by a known value for the investment.

3. We adopt the convention of estimating the expected value of the profitability index, but you might instead estimate the expected values of the profits or of the net present value. The basic modeling approach is the same regardless of the specific measure on which you focus.

4. For example, see Karl Ulrich and Steven Eppinger, "Product Development Economics," in *Product Design and Development*, 4th ed. (New York: McGraw-Hill, 2008).

5. McGrath and MacMillan call this approach *discovery-driven planning*. See Rita G. McGrath and Ian C. MacMillan, "Discovery-Driven Planning," *Harvard Business Review,* July–August 1995.

6. ADIS International; see Karan Girotra, Karl Ulrich, and Christian Terwiesch, "Risk Management in New Product Portfolios: A Study of Late Stage Drug Failures," *Management Science* 53, no. 9 (2007): 1452–1466 for further details.

7. Larrick and Soll provide evidence that averaging opinions works quite well. See R. P. Larrick and J. B. Soll, "Intuitions About Combining Opinions: Misappreciation of the Averaging Principle," *Management Science* 52, no. 2 (2006): 309–310.

8. Panel discussion of the POMS College on Product Innovation and Technology Management, Boston, 2006.

9. This whole category of analysis, which includes the opportunity to kill a project or to invest more, is sometimes called *real options*. For a discussion of real options in the context of innovation, see Rita G. McGrath and Ian C. MacMillan, "Assessing Technology Projects Using Real Options Reasoning," *Technology Management* 43, no. 4 (2000): 35–49.

Chapter 7

1. These examples are from K. Girotra, C. Terwiesch, and K. Ulrich, "New Drug Development at Merck & Co.," case study (Philadelphia: The Wharton School, 2004). All specific numerical values have been disguised to protect proprietary Merck information.

2. The concept of exploration and exploitation was originally developed by James March in his paper "Exploration and Exploitation in Organizational Learning," *Organization Science* 2, no. 1 (1991).

3. Amory B. Lovins, et al., *Winning the Oil Endgame* (Snowmass, CO: Rocky Mountain Institute, 2004).

4. See W. C. Kim and R. Mauborgne, *Blue Ocean Strategy: How to Create Uncontested Market Space and Make Competition Irrelevant* (Boston: Harvard Business School Press, 2005).

5. See S. C. Wheelwright and K. B. Clark, *Revolutionizing Product Development: Quantum Leaps in Speed, Efficiency, and Quality* (New York: Free Press, 1992) and R. G. Cooper, S. J. Edgett, and E. J. Kleinschmidt, *Portfolio Management for New Products*, 2nd ed. (New York: Perseus Books Group, 2001) for more discussions on this topic.

6. Pixar provides a nice description of its movie-making process on its Web site: http://www.pixar.com/howwedoit/index.html.

7. Paul J. H. Schoemaker provides an excellent treatment of scenario analysis and the implications for strategy in "Scenario Planning: A Tool for Strategic Thinking," *Sloan Management Review* (Winter 1995).

Chapter 8

1. John Heilemann, "Reinventing the Wheel," *Time*, December 2, 2001.

2. Steven Kemper, *Code Name Ginger* (Boston: Harvard Business School Press, 2003).

3. The sales figures were made public because of a voluntary recall of the product due to a software problem. See http://www.segway.com/support/recalls.php.

4. The following works have also documented these and other new-category innovations: Peter Golder and Gerard Tellis, "Will It Ever Fly? Modeling the Takeoff of Really New Consumer Durables," *Marketing Science* 16, no. 3 (1997); and Rajshree Agarwal and Barry Bayus, "The Market Evolution and Sales Takeoff of Product Innovations," *Management Science* 48, no. 8 (2002).

5. Although this is a small sample of innovations, these findings are consistent across innovations in many industries. See Golder and Tellis, "Will It Ever Fly?"; Agarwal and Bayus, "Market Evolution and Sales Takeoff"; and Barry Bayus and Rajshree Agarwal, "The Role of Pre-entry Experience, Entry Timing, and Product Technology Strategies in Explaining Firm Survival," *Management Science* 53, no. 12 (2007).

6. James Utterback, *Mastering the Dynamics of Innovation* (Boston: Harvard Business School Press, 1996); Fernando Suarez and Gianvito Lanzolla, "The Half-Truth of First-Mover Advantage," *Harvard Business Review,* April 2005.

7. Suarez and Lanzolla, "Half-Truth."

8. There is some research on the relationship between innovativeness and long-term financial success, but the results are somewhat ambiguous. See, for example, Hee-Jae Cho and Vladimir Pucik, "Relationship Between Innovativeness, Quality, Growth, Profitability, and Market Value," *Strategic Management Journal* 26, no. 6 (2005): 555–575, and Shaker Zahra and Jeffrey G. Corin, "Contextual Influences on the Corporate Entrepreneurship–Performance Relationship: A Longitudinal Analysis," *Journal of Business Venturing* 10, no. 1 (1995): 43–58.

9. The concept of exploration and exploitation was articulated by James March in his paper "Exploration and Exploitation in Organizational Learning," *Organization Science* 2, no. 1 (1991). See also Constantinos C. Markides and Paul A. Geroski, *Fast Second: How Smart Companies Bypass Radical Innovation to Enter and Dominate New Markets* (San Francisco: Jossey-Bass, 2005).

10. Mary Benner and Michael Tushman, "Exploitation, Exploration, and Process Management: The Productivity Dilemma Revisited," *Academy of Management Review* 28, no. 2 (2003).

11. Wesley M. Cohen and Daniel A. Levinthal, "Absorptive Capacity: A New Perspective on Learning and Innovation," *Administrative Science Quarterly* 35, no. 1 (1990). R. Leifer and coauthors provide some practical organizational mechanisms for developing absorptive capacity in *Radical Innovation* (Boston: Harvard Business School Press, 2000).

12. One nice method for identifying tasks, developed by MacMillan and McGrath, is *discovery-driven planning.* To apply discovery-driven planning, you first develop a set of pro forma financial statements and then list the critical assumptions that underlie the financial model. See Rita G. McGrath and Ian C.

MacMillan, "Discovery-Driven Planning," *Harvard Business Review*, July–August 1995. A similar idea is described in H. B. Sykes and D. Dunham, "Critical Assumption Planning," *Journal of Business Venturing* 10, no. 6 (1995): 413.

13. The PERT method and the design structure matrix method are summarized in the chapter on project management in K. T. Ulrich and S. D. Eppinger, *Product Design and Development*, 4th ed. (New York: McGraw-Hill, 2008).

14. See Sungwook Min, Manohar U. Kalwani, and William T. Robinson, "Market Pioneer and Early Follower Survival Risks: A Contingency Analysis of Really New Versus Incrementally New Product-Markets," *Journal of Marketing* 70, no. 1 (2006): 15–33.

15. EZ Pass, http://www.ezpass.com.

16. See, for example, Bronwyn Hall, "Innovation and Diffusion," in *The Oxford Handbook of Innovation*, eds. J. Fagerberg, D. Mowery, and R. Nelson (New York: Oxford University Press, 2005); Everett Rogers, *Diffusion of Innovations*, 4th ed. (New York: Free Press, 1995).

17. Rogers actually uses the term *complexity*, but we have switched the sense of the term to *simplicity* so that all of the five factors are associated with faster rates of diffusion.

Chapter 9

1. K. Girotra, C. Terwiesch, and K. Ulrich, "Idea Generation and the Quality of the Best Idea," working paper, The Wharton School, Philadelphia, 2007.

2. Sommer and Loch provide a detailed discussion of the very closely related distinction between *selectionism* and *learning*. See S. C. Sommer and C. H. Loch, "Selectionism and Learning in Projects with Complexity and Unforeseeable Uncertainty," *Management Science* 50, no. 10 (2004): 1334–1347. The concepts of selection versus learning as related to cascades and whirlpools are closely related to the concepts of exploration and exploitation as developed by J. G. March, "Exploration and Exploitation in Organizational Learning," *Organization Science* 2, no. 1 (1991): 71.

Chapter 10

1. Wikipedia, "Numa Numa," http://en.wikipedia.org/wiki/Numa_numa.

2. O'Connor and DeMartino report on a study of several large established firms and their innovation organizations. They provide a categorization of alternative organizational structures. See G. C. O'Connor and R. DeMartino, "Organizing for Radical Innovation: An Exploratory Study of the Structural Aspects

of Radical Innovation Management," *Journal of Product Innovation Management* 23, no. 6 (2006): 475–497.

3. Even the highly centralized innovation approach at McDonald's has limits. The company does have regional differences in products, offering, for example, beef-free products in India.

4. Quoted in B. Joseph Pine, *Mass Customization: The New Frontier in Business Competition.* (Cambridge: Presidents and Fellows of Harvard College, 1993).

5. Thomas Allen, *Managing the Flow of Technology: Technology Transfer and the Dissemination of Technological Information Within the R&D Organization* (Cambridge, MA: MIT Press, 1977).

Chapter 11

1. This model resembles the very successful and widely used software maturity model (known as the capability maturity model, or CMM) developed at the Software Engineering Institute at Carnegie Mellon University. See http://www.sei.cmu.edu/cmmi/general/.

2. K. E. Weick, "Small Wins: Redefining the Scale of Social Problems," *The American Psychologist* 39, no. 1 (1984): 40–44.

ACKNOWLEDGMENTS

This book draws on the wisdom of many people, and we certainly cannot take credit for all of the ideas in this book. Business professionals, academic colleagues, students, and consulting clients all influenced our thinking.

Our ideas arise to a large extent from our work with executives, whether in the classroom or in our research and consulting. Special thanks go to Brian Kelly at Merck, Peter Terwiesch and Rene Cotting at ABB, Brad Jones at W. L. Gore & Associates, John Levis at Deloitte, Don Richardson at Microsoft, and Stephen Doig at the Rocky Mountain Institute. Our work with TerraPass and Lunar Design also informed our thinking. Many participants in our executive education programs confronted us with the realities of day-to-day innovation management, and their comments are frequently reflected in the book.

We have benefited from inspirational discussions with our academic colleagues. Marshall Fisher, Jerry Wind, and George Day at the Wharton School helped us with the writing and publication process. Christoph Loch from INSEAD has been helpful in a number of ways. Several of his articles pioneered key concepts in this book. He has collaborated with us in research and teaching and has been a close personal friend, supporting us in many ways. Karan Girotra was our doctoral student and is now a professor at INSEAD. He worked with us on Merck's portfolio management challenges and on researching the opportunity identification process, as well as on the development of the Darwinator software.

We gratefully acknowledge the support of the Mack Center for Technological Innovation at the Wharton School. The center's directors, George Day and Harbir Singh, have been generous both with funding and with intellectual support.

Over the last few years, we wrote this book essentially three times, with only the third version surviving to publication. In this process, our own tournament of ideas, thoughtful reviewers were instrumental. We were blessed with exceptionally useful feedback from Barry Bayus, Stephen Doig, David Ellison, Lee Fleming,

Brian Kelly, Laura Kornish, Vish Krishnan, Taylor Randall, Don Richardson, Brian Scallon, Peter Terwiesch, Vit Vasista, and Jerry Wind. Thanks to all of you.

Kirsten Sandberg, executive editor at Harvard Business Press, enthusiastically supported us throughout the creation of the book. Ania Wieckowski, our assistant editor, navigated the publishing process for us. We owe special thanks to George Rausch at Wharton, who controlled various versions of the manuscript, formatted documents, chased down permissions, took photographs, created Web sites, and prepared illustrations. We also would like to thank our development editor, Tim Gray, who improved our exposition and managed to meld two distinct writing styles.

Finally, we owe thanks to our families for their support and patience. Their summer vacations in both 2007 and 2008 were substantially compromised while we struggled to find the time to finish this project.

ABOUT THE AUTHORS

Christian Terwiesch is a professor of operations and information management at the Wharton School of the University of Pennsylvania. He also is the academic director of the Strategic R&D Management Program, a one-week executive education program offered by the Wharton-INSEAD alliance focusing on R&D and innovation. Professor Terwiesch's research is in the area of R&D management and innovation as well as in more traditional topics in operations management such as process analysis and supply chain management. Over the last fifteen years, Professor Terwiesch has collaborated with companies such as Intel, Merck, Dell, Medtronic, BMW, and several large hospitals. He also has cooperated closely with McKinsey, both in research and in teaching. Professor Terwiesch's research has appeared in the leading academic journals, including *Management Science, Marketing Science, Operations Research*, and *Organization Science*. He has also written for practitioner journals, including the *Journal of Product Innovation Management* and *California Management Review*. His textbook, *Matching Supply with Demand: An Introduction to Operations Management* (McGraw-Hill, 2nd ed., 2008), is used in the MBA and executive MBA programs of many business schools around the world. Professor Terwiesch has received numerous teaching awards at Wharton and at INSEAD. He earned his diploma in business and information technology from the University of Mannheim, Germany, and his PhD in management from INSEAD in Fontainebleau, France.

Karl T. Ulrich is the CIBC Professor of Entrepreneurship and e-Commerce at the Wharton School of the University of Pennsylvania. He also holds an appointment as professor of mechanical engineering. His research is focused on innovation, entrepreneurship, and product development. He is the coauthor of *Product Design and Development* (Irwin/McGraw-Hill), a textbook used by over two hundred thousand students worldwide. He is the winner of many teaching awards, including the Anvil Award, the Miller-Sherrerd Award, and the Excellence in Teaching Award at the Wharton School. At Penn, he cofounded the Weiss Tech House and the Integrated Product Design Program, two institutions fostering innovation in the university community. In addition to his academic work, Professor Ulrich has led dozens of innovation efforts for medical devices, tools, computer peripherals, food products, Web-based services, and sporting goods. As a result of this work, he has been granted nineteen patents. Professor Ulrich is a cofounder of Xootr and TerraPass, and he currently serves on the boards of several technology-based companies. Professor Ulrich holds bachelor's, master's, and doctoral degrees in mechanical engineering from the Massachusetts Institute of Technology.